FAITH

THE CHRISTIAN'S HOPE AND SHIELD

Larry Swaim

21st Century Christian

ISBN: 978-0-89098-906-7

Cover design by Jonathan Edelhuber

ACKNOWLEDGMENTS

I wish to thank Cathy Brown and my granddaughter, Hayley Fitzgerald, for their valuable help in editing and proofreading.

Deep appreciation to the late Charlie Walton of Atlanta, Georgia, who many years ago encouraged me to write a book on faith.

DEDICATIONS

To my family—
My children, grandchildren, great-grandchildren,
and to my wife, LaDonna,
who has always encouraged me
to "keep the faith."

TABLE OF CONTENTS

INTRODUCTION

The world has changed dramatically in the recent past. Advancements in science, technology, and medicine have made our lives healthier and have opened incredible communication realities.

In this same period, spiritual and moral values have declined. Christianity is being ridiculed, and Christians all over the world are being persecuted, abused, and even killed.

Militant Islamics have vowed to convert or kill all Jews and Christians. Radical Islamic warriors have already begun their purge of Christianity and other religions. Christians are being persecuted and killed in Africa, Iran, and Syria. Westerners are being beheaded, and Christians in Iraq are having to flee their homes while other Christian men, women, and their children have been killed. Threats of Islamic domination *"caliphate"* come daily from ISIS, Hamas, and al-Qaida.

In the United States, there is another kind of war taking place—a war of ideas and values. Christian morals and values are being attacked from many quarters. God is prohibited in our educational system. Movies, TV, and books ridicule Christianity, depicting Christians in a negative way. Much of today's media emphasis is sacrilegious, demeaning many religions, but targeting Christianity. The Bible is held in contempt or just ignored by many. Abortion, the gay/lesbian "issue," biblical inspiration, and Christian values such as honesty, truthfulness, and sexual morality are being challenged. Christianity is considered of little or no value to millions who were at one time defenders of the faith.

It is not easy to be a Christian today. Many threats and persecutions have created insecurity and doubt, even among passionate Christians. Faith in God—real faith—is our only hope for the future. It is my prayer this book will help you to experience a deeper and more personal faith in God and His Word.

This book is not meant to present scientific or empirical evidence for faith in God, but rather to serve as a reminder for those who once experienced a deep faith but, because of the cares and pressures of the world, have left their first love. We may just need to be reminded why we first believed!

Larry Swaim

DOUBT
The Stairway to Faith

And you, who once were alienated and hostile in mind, doing evil deeds, he has now reconciled in his body of flesh by his death, in order to present you holy and blameless and above reproach before him, if indeed you continue in the faith, stable and steadfast, not shifting from the hope of the gospel that you heard, which has been proclaimed in all creation under heaven, and of which I, Paul, became a minister.

Colossians 1:21-23, ESV

It is unfortunate that many Christians often see doubt as an off-on switch. In our search for simplicity, we readily accept the idea that doubt and faith are mutually exclusive. It may seem logical to us, then, that because we believe, we must suppress and deny any hint of doubt. Yet doubt can be one of the most beneficial conditions of the human spirit if it is used as a stepping stone and is not allowed to become a stumbling block.

At its very outset, Christianity asks a person to accept a God whom he cannot see. It presents a Savior who left this earth nearly twenty centuries ago. It offers the support of an ancient book and a fellowship of peers who have no more insight than anyone else. There should be no surprise when a Christian stops to scratch his head and questions a statement of some item of doctrine or faith.

Doubt should be an understood process among Christians, who are called to a life of faith. However, the opposite is often sadly true. Rather than treating the doubt, many Christians become defensive and attack the doubter. One who is honest enough to admit his sincere concern is often harassed and criticized. When Christians should be extending the hand of fellowship and giving supportive teaching, many find it much easier to chop off an offending member.

Jesus was patient with doubters. He was willing to assist them gently out of their confusion toward certainty. One might wonder why Jesus' people today are so fearful of doubt. Have they forgotten how their own faith may have been born of doubt? Or do they fear that a tolerated uncertainty might soon expose a great bulk of doubt lying white-washed beneath the surface of their own lives? Does Christian apprehension about doubt indicate strength or weakness?

When America was facing the prospect of a terrible depression, President Franklin D. Roosevelt was able to bring clarity to the confusion that plagued so many. He reminded the nation that there was "nothing to fear but fear itself." In much the same way, doubt holds no threat to the truth. It is mainly the fear of doubt that wears away the mortar of Christianity. It is in hypocritically pretending that doubters do not doubt that we erode the foundations of faith.

What Christians need is not just less doubt, but more honesty about our doubt. We need preachers who will say what they believe and church members who will quit saying they believe things that they really doubt. More faith lives in honest doubt than in many of the world's statements of faith.

A World in Doubt

This is an age of anxiety. Doubt and fear contribute to the fact that half the population is on medication, and the other half is wringing their hands. As many as 50 percent of all hospital beds in the United States may be occupied with emotionally-caused illnesses.

Doubts and fears are adding daily recruits to an army of about 17 million alcoholics and problem drinkers in our country alone. Drug abuse is a disease in our society. Suicide is the second leading cause of death among young adults. The number one cause of death in this group, accidents, may hide a considerable number of additional suicides.

Uncertainty is the great motivator of the marketplace. The marketing profession capitalizes on Americans' uncertainty and doubt. When there's a new product to push, it's billed as a panacea, a problem-solver, a sure-cure. We fall right into line and buy their dream machines and personality-props. We readily jump into each new thrill or fad that comes along. Our doubts and fears keep us in the marketplace stocking up on any commodity that promises to add meaning or extension to life, perpetuating the dependency. Doubting the security of the future, many feel the need to tranquilize their present perceptions. We fear the reality of life; we pretend that it isn't really there. Our fears become more dangerous than the reality ever could be.

Among Christians, there are three distinct ways of reacting to doubt. First, there are the *traditionalists*. They want no challenges or shake-ups in the church order. For them, doubts cannot exist. Of necessity, they ignore the questionings and hope they'll go away. The world glances at the traditionalists, snickers at a society of ostriches with heads securely buried in the sand, and goes about its business.

Equally useless to the world are the church folks at the other end of the doubt scale. The *radicals* want to change everything. They would like to do away with Christian symbols and humanize religion. Their preference is for no doctrine, only a social gospel. The world looks disparagingly at the radicals, too. The humanized church has nothing to offer the worry-weary world. The radicals are all doubt and no faith, and they can only promise the world more of the same. It is scant improvement to couch our doubts and fears in religious terminology. What the world needs is answers, not a new set of questions.

Between the traditionalists and the radicals lies the great majority who live with their fears and try to reconcile their doubts. Many may secretly doubt while continuing to give outward signs of assurance and agreement. The fortunate few are mature enough to openly bear their doubts toward eventual resolution.

Compounding the Issue

A significant number of young church workers are leaving the ministry to take secular positions which allow them to deal with problems that frustrate them as ministers. Churches are saying "good riddance" to them when they should be making a more compassionate place for these Christians who harbor a burden of doubt. The church will never be strengthened by only weeding out the weak. Strength comes from strengthening the weak. But the church's own fear of doubt causes it to avoid confrontation with such issues. Jesus always made it clear that the disciples' faith was mustard-seed small, yet He never slammed the door on their growth and maturing processes.

The church has often been unsuccessful in providing men with answers. This has not been because of any weakness or inability in the message presented but because of the weak and diluted methods used in presenting the vital message. It is also caused by the unwillingness of those who claim to be Christians to actually live what they say they love. In many instances, religion has been presented as a sterile list of do's and don'ts. It is often seen as a group of forms and rituals, which have little meaning to the person trying to cope with a complex and competitive society. People are understandably confused when they hear the church preaching a doctrine of selflessness, exclusiveness, and sanctimony. The contradiction between profession and practice is sufficient to raise doubts in most sensitive and perceptive individuals.

Besides the weaknesses of poor communication and an amazing credibility gap, most Christians face a significant ignorance barrier when they get into spiritual realities. "My people are destroyed for lack of knowledge" (Hosea 4:6, NKJV). People generally show more wisdom than to give medical advice or legal counsel without training, yet we fully expect to be able to solve spiritual dilemmas without "cracking the Book." We are unable to answer people who question us because we have such a poor knowledge of the Bible. The apostle Paul points to this problem: "So then faith comes by hearing, and hearing by the word of God" (Romans 10:17, ESV). A genuine faith, one that will stand the test of time and events, is one that is based on a knowledge of God's Word. This knowledge, which is the evidence God offers us for his existence and working in the affairs of men, is scantily understood by many professed Christians. It is difficult to make a defense of faith to others when we have not settled issues in our own minds.

Many pride themselves on the motto: "We speak where the Bible speaks and remain silent where the Bible is silent." This motto makes a generalization which carries with it all the problems of any generalization. Mottoes are useless without appropriate action. Unfortunately, in practice Christians often fail to abide by the principle. A person who hears such a profession and then witnesses our conduct may consequently doubt everything we try to say to him. There is a gap between what we say and what we do.

Doubts are compounded reagularly because so few Christians are able to adequately give an answer concerning their faith.

Rather than answering questions or doubts, we often hide behind clichés such as, "A good Christian will not have doubts." We sometimes act as if a person who questions what we tell him is just trying to be obstinate and stubborn, or we downplay the importance of doctrine or commands.

Admitting Doubt

What are we to do when faced with both our own and others' doubts? The first step in dealing with our own doubts is to admit that they exist, seeking to identify those recognized doubts. We must never be afraid to admit that we doubt. Denying the existence of our doubts succeeds only in preventing us from resolving them. Most Christians assume that having doubts means that their faith is weak, and they are failures as Christians. This isn't necessarily true. It is important to remember that Christianity is a growing process. Each of us must grow in faith continually, always reaching toward a perfect faith. Peter encouraged Christians to "grow in the grace and knowledge of our Lord and Savior Jesus Christ" (2 Peter 3:18).

As Christians grow in faith, our doubts often change. We solve the old problems and move on to more sophisticated ones.The process of a Christian maturing is a continual striving. Until Jesus comes to claim His people, there will be nagging doubts. Satan is far too clever to give up on such an effective weapon. He would rather phase out the defeated doubts and bring on new, more potent ones. Until Jesus returns, we will need patience to live with and overcome doubts, both our own and those of others. Paul characterized this Christian longsuffering when he said, "Brothers, I do not consider that I have made it my own. But one thing I do: forgetting what lies behind and straining forward to what lies ahead, I press on toward the goal, for the prize of the upward call of God in Christ Jesus" (Philippians 3:13, 14, ESV).

The American Heritage Dictionary of the English Language

defines *doubt* as "an unsettled state of opinion concerning the reality or truth of something, a lack of certainty." Doubt is a normal product of a reasoning person. It is necessary for normal human functioning because it allows us to make choices. People who accept everything they are told are considered to be gullible, naïve, and unperceptive.

The Bible accepts doubt as a natural step to faith. Doubt is not rebuked as long as it is honest, sincere, and symptomatic of a searching mind. Many of the psalms reflect a feeling of doubt and questioning. The story of Job recounts one man's painful pilgrimage through a period of great doubt. And yet through all his trials, Job is loved and supported by his proud Heavenly Father. We might even deduce that it was Job's honesty and willingness to question that made him pleasing to God.

The New Testament give us several examples of doubt. The best-known is that of Thomas, one of the twelve apostles. Thomas had the audacity to question whether the man who stood before him claiming to be the risen Christ was actually God's Son. Instead of rebuking Thomas for his doubts, Jesus presented evidence to substantiate His identity. He allowed Thomas to touch His wounds and see that He really was Jesus. The sincerity of Thomas's quest is indicated by his response to the evidence. "My Lord and my God!" exclaimed the apostle in John 20:28. He obviously was not doubting just to be troublesome or intellectual. His honest doubt gave way readily to meaningful evidence.

Another instance of doubt is seen in Nicodemus's questioning of the possibility of a new birth. Jesus patiently explained and illustrated this new principle for the member of the Jewish Sanhedrin. Nicodemus wanted information. He was not a scoffer. Jesus was always patient with sincere seekers of truth. Neither Thomas nor Nicodemus was rebuked for doubting. But the hard-hearted Pharisees who argued with Jesus just to trap Him often felt the sting of His sharp wit.

Few of us would think of characterizing John the Baptist as a doubter. And yet, for all his faith and bold proclamation about Jesus and His divine Sonship, John went through his own periods of doubt. John's concern points up for us a very important distinction regarding kinds of doubt. There are both intellectual doubts and emotional doubts. John sat in Herod's dungeon at the end of a fiery and provocative preaching career. He reflected on the words he had preached, the hearts he had touched, and the way he had prepared. He knew that by all intellectual evidence, Jesus had to be the Messiah for whom he had been preparing the people. John did not doubt intellectually—he suffered from the emotional stresses of uncertainty and not being in touch. He sent his disciples to Jesus for reassurance.

Jesus answered John's doubts, and He is able to answer the information lapses that cause our doubts today. John's disciples had only to observe Jesus at work, healing the sick and preaching good news to the poor. The doubt-dispelling facts were written all over Jesus' daily activities. When these kinds of actions were reported to the imprisoned John, his emotional confidence was bolstered to the strong position that his factual understanding had occupied all along.

Often, people will be thoroughly familiar with the scriptural accounts of God's power. They read the Bible, but they are tripped up concerning the miracles, the six-day creation, the virgin birth, and other matters of faith versus doubt, and because their emotional and intellectual faith components get out of step with each other, they discount the whole matter.

One of the most needed lessons among human beings is the ability to be patient with ourselves. We must learn to give ourselves time to grow instead of demanding immediate maturity from ourselves at the outset. The same Peter who doubted and nearly drowned trying to walk on the water later preached the first Christian sermon and remained a tower of faith to the early church.

We must remember that this life embraces only the beginning stages of our lives as Christians. It is only the staging area for the great things that will be when eternity begins. The small quantities we are able to grasp and struggle with under the present limitations will look insignificant when we see God as He really is. Robert Leighton beautifully remarks, "It is but little that we can receive here, some drops of joy that enter into us; but there we shall enter into joy, as vessels put into a sea of happiness."

As Christians, we must discipline ourselves to learn to live briefly with our doubts, but not to serve them. We must allow them to run their courses and be swallowed up in faith. We must make the significant distinction between faith and expectation, trusting the Lord to do what He will, but never putting Him to the test. The habit of suggesting human hoops for God to jump through to prove Himself and dispel our doubts is shortsighted. The God who would have to run around proving His existence and power to His people would, in so doing, deny His own supremacy.

Christians need to be as patient as possible with those who are experiencing doubt. There is, however, a problem of ethics involved. A distinction must be made between "patience with doubters" and "encouragement of false teaching." Church leaders must never sacrifice the well-being of the church by being foolishly tolerant of those who would occupy a pulpit each Sunday and preach what they do not believe. Preachers should not be encouraged or allowed to live a lie, claiming to be something they do not want to be. Many modern ministers rationalize by saying that they are willing to use the symbols that the people understand and need even though they personally can no longer accept those symbols. This is wrong. There is no justification for lying, especially for living a lie. Yet this is how any minister must live if he cannot believe in God, Jesus, the virgin birth, and the resurrection, and must regularly stand before a congregation which believes these doctrines. By letting them think that he believes in them, he comes under the strict condemnation which the Scriptures place upon false teachers and "wolves in sheeps' clothing" (Matthew 7:15). No one effectively teaches that which he does not believe. His doubts are sure to be communicated along with the certainties. Those who do not believe in God or who do not know whether God exists should honestly state that belief and suffer whatever consequences may come to them as a result. How arrogant and presumptuous it is for any minister to say, "I can't tell the congregation the truth about what I believe because they are too naïve to accept it at this time, or too naïve to understand what I understand." The believers are much happier and more consistent in what they believe than are the faithless theologians who feel so sorry for them.

To doubt is normal. To wonder is natural and understandable. We should not criticize or condemn a person simply because he harbors doubts, or because he wonders about some particular point of Christianity. Additionally there is no way to justify lying in the pulpit. The end does not justify the means. Faith must come from sincere lips to have the ring of truth about it.

The first step in overcoming the disabling grip of religious doubt is to be honest—to admit the existence of our uncertainties. Lying does not solve our problems, but it *does* create new problems. As the psalmist wrote, "How can men be wise? The only way to begin is by reverence for God. For growth in wisdom comes from obeying his laws. Praise his name forever" (Psalm 111:10, TLB).

Opening the Mind

Possibly 50 percent of the children raised in Christian homes either leave the church entirely or place it far down on their list of priorities when they are grown. Many of them turn to agnostic philosophies, which they feel better fit their needs. One of the causes of such rejection of Christianity is the failure of the church to come to grips with normal doubts. Each person has doubts about himself and his relationship to his fellow man and to God. If the church refuses to admit the doubts' existence and to attempt solutions, it is asking for mass defections by young people going out on their own.

Once we have doubts and uncertainties out in the open, there is another task immediately before Christians. Opening the minds of people and churches is difficult but essential. It requires security and courage, two attributes often in short supply with doubters. Even so, it is imperative that a willingness to work with doubters be established. In most religious arguments, there are two or more sides knocking heads with each other, neither intending to give an inch. When everybody is talking and nobody is listening, the stage is set for the compounding of doubt rather than the resolution of it. When two minds meet, they must each be willing to accept the possibility that the other may be right. More often, religious discussions are encounters between one dominator and one submitter. The result may be called conversation, but it may be closer to brow-beating.

The next step in analyzing and eliminating doubts is to see what they are and why they exist. Christians should prayerfully ask the Lord's help in this analysis and in supplying a means to resolve the doubts. We should study the Scriptures to try to find answers. The Bible teaches that each of us "Do your best to present yourself to God as one approved, a worker who has no need to be ashamed, rightly handling the word of truth" (2 Timothy 2:15, ESV).

It is always a good idea to get help with a problem. The old saying about "two heads are better than one" is good advice. It would certainly be advisable to discuss the problem with mature Christians and study with them. Small prayer and study groups are ideal for this. They allow one to utilize the thinking and resources of group dynamics. Such a situation probably will reveal that others have had similar doubts, which they have already resolved. Their resolutions can be an aid to you. It helps a person to gain encouragement and strength to realize that he is not alone in his doubts.

Once the doubts are out in the open, the mind is clear, and we have shared the need with God and our fellow Christians, we are well on the way toward finding a solution. With the mind open and willing to consider all facts, the doubts are in their proper perspective and will soon yield to the evidence.

Considering the Evidence

It is true that much of Christianity is not subject to absolute proof and must, therefore, be accepted on the basis of faith. Yet it is not a blind faith, that is, a faith totally devoid of evidence. There is enough evidence to allow one to accept Christ and Christianity. There is risk involved—as there is in any venture of faith. Christians should always recognize and openly discuss those risks. Jesus never tried to conceal the risks of discipleship. He encouraged His listeners to count the cost before following Him. It is dishonest to misrepresent the nature of Christianity for the sake of an easy conversation.

Christ, on one occasion, was asked to prove whether He was indeed the Messiah. Instead of answering directly, He asked those who stood by to consider the evidence of His works. He allowed this evidence to verify His identity. As Jesus' people, we must not just criticize those who express doubts. These doubts present an opportunity to present the evidence. Rather than letting the evidence sufficiently answer the doubts, we often take the easier course of criticizing the brother who has confided in us.

When you are confronted with someone in doubt, as a Christian, you must remember to show love. It is essential to encourage the doubter to ask questions because he may already fear rejection. He may be afraid of ridicule or suppose that there is no answer.

Help him to keep searching, for the answer does exist. He simply has not found it yet.

If people sense your interest in helping them and your respect for their search for truth, they will be more willing to ask the questions that are bothering them. Someone has put it quite succinctly: "People don't care how much you know until they know how much you care."

Never feel that you must protect the Bible. The Bible is truth and is certainly capable of protecting itself. It offers its own best defenses. When a person is truly interested in finding an answer to his problems, he will find it in the Bible. Through the study of this ageless book, his faith will be strengthened.

Remember to pray for understanding. The Bible instructs us to pray for wisdom—wisdom to cope with our problems and to answer our doubts.

Doubting Openly

Often, Christians have dealt in cowardly and childish ways with the doubts among us. Rather than meeting and beating them, we have pretended that they did not exist. Doubts don't go away when ignored; they grow and multiply. Unless we want to repeat the painful mistakes of the past, we must learn to get our doubts out into the open and work on them together like brothers. Doubts ignored will, like cancer, slowly eat away at the very heart of life. Much of the sickness of the church today can be directly traced to the damage done by doubts that everyone agreed did not exist.

Sad Results of Unresolved Doubts

There are consequences resulting from unresolved doubts about the existence of God, the divinity of Jesus, or the infallibility of Scripture. If there is no God and no absolute standard, then who is to say what is right or wrong? It becomes a matter of everyone doing what is right in his own mind.

How is anyone to know what is right and what is wrong? What are the criteria to be used to judge good and evil, right and wrong? If there is not a God and the Bible isn't reliable, then who is to say that even love is the ultimate good? Who's to say that hate is not superior to love? Who is to say that murder or stealing or prejudice or bigotry are wrong?

The basis of all social justice and morality is rooted in the concept of an absolute standard. There must be some absolute right and wrong. Yet for anyone who does not believe in God or absolute truth, what basis can there be for his authority to believe in love, justice, goodness, or any other virtue he may claim? Some would like to say that they are working for the humanitarian virtues of life. But if there is no God and no absolute standard such as the Bible, then it is a matter of "might makes right," and the world we live in will be dominated by the greatest force.

We are reaping the effects of teaching away all our absolute standards. Some teachers have convinced many young people that there is no God and no absolute standard. Their minds, working faster than computers, reason that if there is no God or absolute standard, then they have no responsibilities to their parents. The students then reject any responsibility to civil government, because it is the Bible that teaches obedience to those who have the rule over us. Finally, why should anyone accept a responsibility to be moral? It is the Bible that forbids adultery, lying, and stealing.

If the Bible is not true, then none of these criteria are binding. Some teachers have also convinced young people that they came into being through some quirk in nature, evolved over several million years, and possess no eternal souls. When one takes away God and the absolute authority of His Word, there are no guideposts left. We have no way of knowing what is good and what is bad.

Doubt is rampant among Christians. And the best way to make

it spread is to continue hiding it and pretending it doesn't exist. The only way to get rid of deadly doubt is through recognizing its presence, opening our minds, and bringing an understanding and compassionate fellowship together against the doubts among us.

I am not defending doubt, and I would not want you to feel that I am encouraging anyone to hold doubts. This is not the case. Doubt, fear, and worry are cripplers of man and should be overcome as quickly as possible. Nevertheless, doubts are normal and can only be overcome through a deepening faith which can only be achieved through a greater knowledge of God as He is revealed to us through His Word and through an application of the principles of God's Word to our lives.

Christianity will succeed or fail according to the degree of faith its followers possess. The failures of Christianity today can be traced directly to the lukewarm, indifferent, complacent faith exemplified by so many Christians. Those who claim Christ must develop strong, dynamic, catalytic faith in what the Word teaches. They must know that God loves them, is concerned about them, and has provided a rich way of life here and a better way of life hereafter. The evidence upon which to base such a faith is available. We must examine the evidence God reveals to us about His nature and His purpose for our lives.

I sincerely pray that you will lay aside your doubts, fear, and worries and place your confidence in God, Who is able to raise you above your doubts. Amen.

Food For Thought

1. Have you ever doubted some point of faith?

2. How did Jesus deal with honest doubters?

3. How does doubt affect us in other areas of life?

4. As Christians, what choices do we have in reacting to doubt?

5. Should we admit our doubts?

6. What are some New Testament examples of people who doubted?

7. What should we do to help resolve our doubt?

8. What are some consequences of our unresolved doubts?

FAITH
Born of Doubt

So flee youthful passions and pursue righteousness, faith, love, and peace, along with those who call on the Lord from a pure heart. Have nothing to do with foolish, ignorant controversies; you know that they breed quarrels. And the Lord's servant must not be quarrelsome but kind to everyone, able to teach, patiently enduring evil, correcting his opponents with gentleness. God may perhaps grant them repentance leading to a knowledge of the truth, and they may come to their senses and escape from the snare of the devil, after being captured by him to do his will.

2 Timothy 2:22-26, ESV

Faith is one of those words that we have ceased to hear. It is, of course, still in common use but it is one of those words that, unfortunately, goes rather automatically in one ear and out the other. Faith is a word chock-full of meaning for every person, yet it has been overused and carelessly abused until it has nearly ceased to communicate deep meanings.

Christians live by faith in a world of faithlessness. Yet, we call it many other things to avoid confusion with the faith that we all assume belongs only to religion. The faiths we can hold quite openly and proudly in church on Sunday seem to melt quickly on Monday into a sort of mystical fairy tale realm, which is unrelated to the real world.

Many Christians are quite willing to maintain a double standard of faith. We can abide some gigantic faith loads as long as we are just talking. But when the chips are down and it's time to live our faith, then the excuses begin to flow. Jesus often referred to this hypocritical human trait. He reserved His worst condemnation for the Pharisees, whose specialty was talking one faith and living another.

Christians' primary faith problem is not that we fail to articulate—we have let fly volumes of verbiage about our beliefs. But our great need is for some inner voice that will stop us in mid-action and remind us what we ought to do if we really believe what we claim to believe.

If Christians were more honest, we might be a little more hesitant about laying claim to great faith. As James tells us, the real measure of faith is the kind of behavior it causes (James 2:17). As we grow in maturity in Jesus, we can learn to let our actions show that we believe. Otherwise, we spend our time trying to understand the blatant discrepancies between what we say we believe and what we demonstrate that we believe.

Faith is not just an elusive commodity; it is the very core of commitment. If a person truly believes in Jesus, that faith will automatically make itself known. On the other hand, if true faith is absent, all the religious legal systems in the world will not bring one's life under God's control.

What is Faith?

If faith is so important, what is it? How do we get it? And how do we act when we possess it? God does not leave us in the dark on these questions. He provides the answers through His Word. And, interestingly enough, the very act of understanding and accepting the Word is the initial step of faith. In God's divine wisdom He gives us faith as a by-product of the search for faith.

In the Bible, God not only gives readers a definition of faith,

He follows the definition with examples of historic faithful lives. The entire eleventh chapter of Hebrews is devoted to the subject of faith. Hebrews 11:1 defines faith, "Now faith is the assurance of things hoped for, the conviction of things not seen" (ESV). Phillips translates the same passage this way: "Faith means putting our full confidence in the things we hope for and it means being certain of the things we cannot see."

Two words of prime importance in this passage from Hebrews are *substance* and *evidence*. *Substance* was used as a legal term in Jesus' day. It referred to the sum total of documents that could be assembled to prove a person's identity. This substance would give the person the right to an inheritance. If, for instance, a wealthy man died leaving an only son, the son would need to prove his identity in order to receive his rightful inheritance. To do this, he would gather all of the evidence or *substance*, as it is called in the New Testament, that proved his identity. The substance would then be presented to the magistrate or judge. On the basis of its authenticity, the inheritance would be granted.

So the Bible becomes the substance of proof, the evidence, to the faithful. Through faith we are able to bridge life's uncertain gaps and possess the confidence to act. It was through their faith in life after death that the early Christian martyrs were able to astound their murderers with confidence in the face of death. The simple, but critical, difference between two individuals may be the fact that one believes and the other does not.

The everyday word *belief* is a combination of two ancient Anglo-Saxon words. The combination itself has a two-fold meaning, filled with deep significance. The two root words are *be*, to live or exist, and *lifan*, which conveys the thought of accordance. Thus, to believe means literally to live in accordance with something.

Some are accustomed to the idea that "belief" is simple mental assent to a truth. But its root leads us on to action; that which the mind accepts, the will must obey. We do not truly believe, therefore, unless the conviction is manifested in our behavior. Thus understood, "belief" and its great synonym "faith" mean not only to have trust, but to manifest that trust by practical commitment.

What Is Not Faith?

True faith cannot be mental assent alone. There are many who claim faith in Jesus. They will tell you readily that Jesus is God's Son. Yet their faith is not sufficient to cause them to obey God. James teaches that even the devils believe, and they, at least, support their faith by a minimal action...they tremble.

Neither is faith some sort of magic. The years of sermonic emphasis on faith have perhaps promoted the prevailing idea that faith is a sort of spiritual hocus-pocus, which is possessed by preachers and a privileged few. Yet the truth is that faith is a fact of human nature. It perhaps confuses us because of its simplicity. We are uncomfortable in the presence of things that are too easy, so we have added to faith all kinds of traditional stipulations. Simply stated, if you believe, it will be evident to those who watch what you do.

Faith is not blind acceptance of unsubstantiated evidence. Many people say that they cannot be Christians because Christians must function on "blind faith." Not true. Our faith is based upon evidence. "The heavens declare the glory of God, and the sky above proclaims his handiwork" (Psalm 19:1, ESV). We have but to look at the beauty of nature, the orderliness of the universe, and the mystery of life and death to know that there is a power greater than man.

Naturalist William Beebe once told of a visit that he made to Theodore Roosevelt at Sagamore Hill. After an evening's discussion, the two men walked onto the sprawling lawn and looked up into the night sky. They competed to see who could first identify the pale bit of light-mist near the upper left-hand corner of the Great Square of Pegasus, and then Roosevelt recited, "That is the Spiral Galaxy of Andromeda. It is one of a hundred million galaxies. It is 2,500,000 light-years away. It consists of one hundred billion suns, many larger than our own sun." The two men then stood silently for a moment. Finally Theodore Roosevelt grinned and said, "Now, I think we are small enough. Let's go to bed."

Faith is not simple mental assent. It is not magic. It is far more logical than "blind faith." But, on the other hand, faith is not perfect knowledge and understanding. Many Christians feel like faith-failures because they know there are still doubts that blemish their understanding. Faith, by its very nature, must have some uncertain parts. Otherwise, we are not talking about faith, but fact. And that has not been promised until the end of this world.

How Do You Get Faith?

There are many Christians who want a deeper faith yet are not sure of how to get it. The answer is fairly obvious once we shake loose from the magical concepts of faith. The faiths that we hold in the everyday world come to us through three regular stages. First, we accept the idea because it is related to us from some trusted individual, perhaps a parent. Second, we strengthen the faith as we reflect on it in our own minds. And finally, our faith is confirmed when we try the faith in practice and discover that it works.

In Christianity, we learn the fact of faith from God's written Word, the Bible. It is true that we can sense God's existence through the world He has created. Still, we can find out more about God from the Bible than from the universe in general, just as you can find out more about a man by listening to his conversation than by looking at a house he has built.

We can look to the internal evidence of God's Word. From an in-depth study of His Word, we can arrive at the conclusion that the evidence demands faith in God's existence. Our study of the Bible and life-testing its principles confirms our faith in God and in the Bible as His Word.

The Bible itself speaks to the problem of faith and identifies the source of faith. "So then faith comes by hearing, and hearing by the word of God" (Romans 10:17, NKJV). The only place to get deep, satisfying faith is from a knowledge of God's Word. Faith comes by listening to God.

It is true that our faith is supplemented and confirmed by science and nature. Yet neither science nor nature is able to supply us with the information we need to follow God. These two avenues are only supplementary to a basic knowledge of God's Word. Only the Bible can give us the information necessary for a sustaining, satisfying, deep faith. The evidence we need to build our faith in God is contained in the Bible. Saving faith, satisfying faith, comes from an understanding of God's Word and an obedience to that Word.

In the Old Testament, we learn how God dealt with ancient man. He always meant what He said. He never issued a commandment or made a promise that He did not expect His people to keep or was not willing to keep Himself. Both Old and New Testament examples show that God has always been true to His Word. Therefore, on the basis of God's Word, the Bible, we can know our future. Christians know that because God has kept His promises in the past, He will keep them in the future. Our faith in God, in Christ, and in the Bible, is based upon the evidence of the past. We have confidence that God will keep His promises to us in the future. As Paul stated, "I know whom I have believed, and I am convinced that he is able to guard until that Day what has been entrusted to me" (2 Timothy 1:12, ESV).

Faith, then, means surrendering our total being to God as a

result of the evidence we have for His existence. It is complete confidence in God and His Son because of the evidence and our evaluation of it.

Christians believe in God because of the overwhelming evidence, the evidence of nature and history. Further, our faith has been confirmed by the infallibility of God's words and His providence working in our own lives. Faith means that we consider all the evidence and, on the basis of the evidence, we commit our lives to God for the future.

The Ancient Examples

Hebrews 11 has been described as the great faith chapter of the Bible. Listed in Hebrews 11 are men and women who have demonstrated the quality of faith that God wants each of us to have.

> By faith Moses, when he was grown up, refused to be called the son of Pharaoh's daughter, choosing rather to be mistreated with the people of God than to enjoy the fleeting pleasures of sin. He considered the reproach of Christ greater wealth than the treasures of Egypt, for he was looking to the reward (Hebrews 11:24-26, ESV).

Moses was looking in two directions. One direction was toward the pomp, splendor, and pharaohship of Egypt. The other was toward suffering and hardship with God's people. It was only by faith that Moses could have made his heroic decision. This decision was made recognizing that God would keep His promises to him. Moses yielded himself completely to the promise of God that He would use him as a deliverer and that He would always protect him. He demonstrated his complete and total confidence in God and believed that God would be sufficient to meet his every need.

Moses was manifesting the same confidence that had led his ancestor, Noah, to build an ark before it even started to rain.

> By faith Noah, being warned by God concerning events as yet unseen, in reverent fear constructed an ark for the saving of his household. By this he condemned the world and became an heir of the righteousness that comes by faith (Hebrews 11:7, ESV).

Noah believed God's promises concerning the destruction of the world by flood. He did not simply give mental assent. He believed completely enough to hammer the nails and endure the ridicule. It is essential, then, that our faith be the kind that is active, dynamic, and obedient.

Many generations before Moses, Abraham was demonstrating the kind of action which would earn him the title "father of the faithful."

> By faith Abraham obeyed when he was called to go out to a place that he was to receive as an inheritance. And he went out, not knowing where he was going (Hebrews 11:8, ESV).

The complete confidence Abraham demonstrated in going into the strange land proved that he had completely given himself to God. Not until our faith is backed up by action and complete obedience to God's will is it the kind of faith God wants us to have.

A second reference to Abraham's faith gives us some insight into the depth of this man's faith.

> By faith Abraham, when he was tested, offered up Isaac, and he who had received the promises was in the act of offering up his only son... (Hebrews 11:17, ESV).

What a difficult test for Abraham! Isaac was the son that had been promised to him in his old age. He had been told that through Isaac all nations of the earth should be blessed. Yet God was now asking him to take the life of this son of promise. Abraham could not understand. There seemingly was no logic to it. Yet the Bible says he prepared the altar. He raised the dagger and was ready to take his son's life, but God stayed his hand. There follows a statement that shows us why God had put Abraham to the test. God's reaction to Abraham's faith was simply to say, "Now I know." Now, I know that you are my faithful servant!

Faith In Our Time

Tests come to us in our lives, too. We often fail to pass them with the faith of Abraham. Sometimes God asks us, through His Word, for certain acts of obedience for which we may see no reason and cannot logically explain. It may be nothing more than a test of our faith in Him. Faith alone or without doing the will of God is a dead faith. It will not save. Noah could not have been saved without building the ark nor Moses without making the proper decision to follow God. Abraham was a man who shared all the humanity and temptation that we can know in our time. But Abraham could not have been saved without going into that far country or having been willing to offer up Isaac. The demands of faith may often seem overwhelming. Yet the faith that brought the demands will supply the sustenance to serve God. If we have faith, we cannot refuse God.

Faith On the Move

One of the most tragic mistakes of many Christians is to try to put faith in a test tube. In the effort to isolate and refine faith, the reality is lost. As James explained to his first-century followers, faith without works is dead (James 2:17). He was pointing to the obvious fact that faith can only be seen and recognized by what is being done in the tangible world.

This fact has provided fuel for the enduring controversies among theologians regarding the relationship between faith and works. There have arisen the "faith only" camps and even "works only" camps. Perfectly sane human beings, who would not attempt to discuss *personality* apart from *performance*, will try to draw the thin line between faith and the works it prompts.

It is possible to spend a lot of time talking about steam apart from the steam engine, but it is not likely that much reality and a true description can ever be given to steam until a steam engine is wheeled in. Show the student the steam at work in the engine, and you can save many words of explanation. Christians will do well to stop explaining faith to the world around them and start demonstrating it. Show them the faith of Jesus Christ working in Christians, and you can save yourself a lot of needless sermonizing.

Many Christians fall into the temptation of sharing their faith and doctrine in a rather defensive manner. Rather than living aggressively, we often find it more comfortable to preach defensively. The major efforts seem devoted to the maintenance of the status quo. The church needs to take the offensive. We must not simply build church buildings as forts in which to isolate ourselves and peer at the big, bad world outside. Christ demands of His disciples to "Go into all the world and proclaim the gospel to the whole creation" (Mark 16:15, ESV). We are not to become of the world, but we must move out into the world if we are to demonstrate our faith.

Keep the Faith
Since the earliest days of God's dealings with mankind, there has been a continuing parade of man's efforts to come up with a better system of faith. Rather than accept the wisdom of our Maker, some Christians seem driven to reinterpret the old truths or re-word the faith of our fathers. Some assume everything becomes more relevant through the process of being modernized. For some reason, man likes his religion but, century after century, he keeps trying to work God out of it!

Godless religion has been tested again and again ever since the snake told Eve that God was not telling her the truth. You may feel that God is not being taken out of religion. But stop for a moment, and think about the past. Who began the "God is dead" philosophies: the atheists or the theologians? It was begun by philosophy and theology teachers in church-related schools. Remember, also, that it was our religious leaders who helped popularize the phrase "the new morality."

Those who feel today that we need a new religion, a new morality, a new philosophy, are basing their belief on the theory that man has changed, that he is not the same man he once was, that he has been emancipated from the old, barbaric man of past civilizations.

Sometimes in human pride, we feel that we have elevated ourselves to a new plateau of achievement. We have changed everything around us; buildings are taller and more elaborate. We go higher in the sky than we have ever gone before, deeper in the sea than ever before. We travel faster; we have more conveniences. We have changed everything—everything except ourselves, for man today is as he has always been. We are separated from Adam by only the years. We still have the same wants, needs, and desires, and we still wrestle with the same personal problems. We are still confronted with the same dilemmas.

Man has not changed! He has changed his environment somewhat, but he has not changed himself. Anger, fear, distrust, greed, and hatred are still the ravages of our civilization, and love, kindness, compassion, and faith are still the hope for mankind.

If man's disease has not changed, then we should not change the *remedy*. The problem of mankind is still "missing the mark," and sin is still as hurtful as ever. There are no new sins, and none of the old ones have been removed. The message of faith remains unchanged more than two thousand years later because man remains unchanged.

Food For Thought

1. Is there a difference in your Sunday faith and your Monday faith? If so, what?

2. How does your faith make itself known?

3. What is your definition of faith?

4. How does the Bible define faith?

5. How can we develop a strong faith?

6. What are some helpful examples of faith?

7. What do all these examples have in common?

8. What hinders your faith?

Commitment
The Result of Faith

For I am already being poured out as a drink offering, and the time of my departure has come. I have fought the good fight, I have finished the race, I have kept the faith. Henceforth there is laid up for me the crown of righteousness, which the Lord, the righteous judge, will award to me on that Day, and not only to me but also to all who have loved his appearing.

2 Timothy 4:6-8, ESV

We live in an age of gaps. There's a credibility gap, a generation gap, and the ever-present communication gap. We've grown accustomed to taking everything with a grain of salt. "Growing up" has almost become synonymous with "becoming skeptical." A whole new school of psychology has developed— the behaviorists who tell us, "Don't talk to me about what you *believe*...just let me measure what you do."

The world has no shortage of professors of faith. What the world does lack is a body of the committed who will let their actions speak for them. The outward signs of religion are abundant. Yet, just as prevalent are the signs of unbelief. Pick up your daily newspaper. On one page, you will marvel at increased church attendance, elaborate new buildings, aggressive new mission projects. But turn the page, and you are right back in the increasing crime rate, the mounting disrespect for law and order, and man's inhumanity to man. If ever there was a society determined to have both worlds, it is this one.

The problem may not lie in our doctrine. Many are saying all the right words. The problem may be one of conversion. A number of people claiming to be Christians have been convinced; they still need to be converted.

The term *conversion* literally means "a turning." It is used in the Bible to describe the absolute reversal of lifestyle, which results from a new set of life's principles. The old methods of making life's transactions became obsolete when Jesus ushered in a new perspective. In the first century, conversion meant change. Today it often means a marginal acceptance of a group of religious facts with the assumption that they won't interfere too much with daily life.

It is a wise movement which makes a distinction between nominal membership and true commitment. With commitment, all things are possible. With mere nominal members, it will soon die of its own weight. Goethe said that the primary theme in the history of the world is the conflict between belief and unbelief. He was referring to the power of commitment. We love the stories of dramatic heroism because they illustrate how one person committed to an ideal can indeed make a difference in the course of his world. We have seen it in business, battle, and boycotts—commitment can make water run uphill.

Humanistic Confidence

There has never been a time when people were so certain of their ability to achieve any goal; and yet at the same time, we are so thoughtless about the goals we should pursue. We have vague dreams of creating a brave new world in which there will be no hunger, no pain, no sorrow, no regrets. As each day passes, we are increasingly assured of our ability to build such a world. But our goal remains hazy and nebulous. We are often a bewildered, lost society in a hurry to go somewhere, but we cannot make up our minds where we want to go.

Ours is an age in which it is becoming increasingly difficult for the individual to know where he is going. It reminds us of Don Quixote's squire Sancho Panza, who is said to have jumped on his donkey and ridden off "in all directions at once." The weakness of our age is its lack of committed individuals in general and committed Christians in particular.

The Church's Inferiority Complex

The lack of total, motivating commitment produces a grave weakness in God's church. Proclaiming itself to be the "handiwork of God," it secretly doubts its own potency. Outwardly claiming to lead the lost to safety, it inwardly nurses its own feelings of inferiority. The church is weak because of a lack of commitment resulting from a lack of true faith.

The weakness of the church is certainly not external. Outwardly the church appears prosperous. To the casual observer, Christianity speaks of growth and conquest. But inwardly the church is sick from under-commitment. Throughout history, whenever the church has faltered, it has been the result of weakness from within, not challenge from without. In fact, in times of oppression, the church reached its greatest heights. It withstood because of strong Christians. They were demonstrating their commitment of faith.

Today, many Christians have sold themselves to the world. Or perhaps the world has "bought" Christianity. In any event, the price seems to have been cheap. Challenges to commitment like "Take up your cross and follow me" seem quaint to a church that awards its faithful preacher a new Cadillac and pays him a six-figure salary. What does a new Cadillac say about our priorities?

There has been one other civilization whose situation was similar to ours. We've all heard the historical reports of the conditions that brought about Rome's downfall. But isn't it curious? Societies become outwardly religious at the height of their moral decline. The lack of commitment on the part of many Christians is symptomatic of a deep and prevailing cancer in the church. Both Christians and the country as a whole need to take a look at our commitments and priorities. Jesus said that it is impossible for a man to serve two masters, and history shows that the same applies to nations. Abortion, the gay rights movement, churches redefining sin all came in this age of record church attendance.

Ultimate Victory

"When the Son of Man comes, will he find faith on the earth?" (Luke 18:8, ESV). Whether or not He does depends to a large extent on us and the validity of our commitment to His cause. Commitment, not just belief, makes the real difference. The key to the Christian life lies in commitment in every realm of life. The present challenge is for the church to get into the lead of life. The world was changed in the first century because it craved the power of commitment demonstrated by the Christians.

The Deciding Factor

Commitment is pivotal to any movement. The world today is torn between two basic philosophies of life. It always has been so. The world will ultimately make its choice between God and godlessness on the basis of the commitment it finds in the representatives of each philosophy.

Commitment is more than a concept; it is a responsibility. America has paid a fearful price both in human lives and natural resources because of commitments to foreign nations. We certainly have the ability to follow through on commitments. We need only to straighten out our thinking on the goals worth our sacrifices.

In recent years we have been repeatedly shocked by people who commit suicide to draw attention to something they believe in. It is a dramatic demonstration of the power of commitment, even if it is misguided.

Our nation, and consequently the world, is being drained of billions of dollars each year because of a commitment to defense. Christians are faced with a question of far-reaching implications: "Can Christians match the world's commitment? Can Christians supply missionaries for soldiers? Living sacrifices in place of burning bodies? Food for the starving, as well as fuel for missiles?" In India, ten thousand people die every day of malnutrition. In a world where more than a billion people are forever hungry, the challenge to commitment is of supreme importance.

We've got the money. That makes the question of Christian commitment just a little embarrassing. The question of commitment cannot be ignored or swept under the rug. Where is the proof of our commitment? Of our faith?

Paul lived in a society similar to ours. The Roman Empire of the first century was extremely religious. Every city was crowded with temples and shrines. Men of high and low degree sought to ease their troubled spirits by religious practice. If a pollster could have taken a man-on-the-street survey in ancient Rome, he would have found a high percentage of self-proclaimed servants of the gods.

It was a religious age, but also an immoral age. It was a time that was eaten out at the soul; responsibility, family loyalty and solidarity, and integrity, the solid virtues that had once made the Roman Empire feared and honored throughout the known world, had all at once disappeared, having been swept away in a vast flood of lust and lying, immorality and indulgence.

The same fascination with obscenity, the lack of reliable responsibility, the same selfish pursuit of comfort and convenience that is known today, was known in Paul's day. In the opening words of his letter to the church in Rome, Paul analyzed the reason for the situation. He looked, on one hand, at the religious intensity present, and on the other, at the vain imaginations. He questioned how man could believe in God and produce such an immoral world. The flaw, Paul concluded, was in their religion. Yes, it was their religion that produced their immorality. "For although they knew God, they did not honor him as God or gave thanks to him" (Romans 1:21, ESV). They lacked commitment. They talked one religion and lived another.

The mortality rate in Christianity is staggering. A high percentage of those who become Christians will eventually leave the church. There are also many who, after becoming Christians, never make a complete break and leave the church altogether, but have little commitment. They may even be considered by many to be faithful Christians.

The church at Laodicea was criticized by Jesus, not because of gross immorality, but because of indifference. Indifference, or complacency, accurately describes too many twenty-first century Christians. Christ wants us to be energetic, aggressive, devoted, Christians. This can be accomplished only through commitment produced by faith.

Jesus offers us abundant life. Commitment makes the difference. Christians have no monopoly on commitment, but we do have an eternal objective. We are not guaranteed success here. The only guarantee we have is the ultimate victory of Christianity. We shouldn't be astonished at the amazing growth of the early church. The early church grew because of its deep commitment and its willingness to sacrifice. Only an identical commitment in our day will produce similar results. Commitment to Jesus is the secret to successful living.

Traitors and fair-weather friends always qualify for bad-guy awards. We rarely like things watered down or half-safe. We like people and things to be 100 percent sincere and true-blue.

In this day of hard-sell and calculated deception, it is refreshing to hear the words of One who would accept no partial commitment. Jesus spoke to a basic human need when He said, "No one can serve two masters" (Matthew 6:24, ESV). Centuries before the first psychiatrist talked about self-deception or divided loyalties, Jesus had the problem pegged—indecision will tear one apart. Be committed.

Food For Thought

1. How does faith cause us to act?
2. How is faith in ourselves sometimes confused with true faith in God?
3. How does our weak faith affect our Christian mission?
4. How was Rome's world similar to ours?
5. How is misguided faith and commitment seen in our world today?
6. Why is our Christian mortality rate so high?
7. What is key to an abundant life here on earth?
8. How is your faith?

KNOWLEDGE OF GOD
The Beginning of Faith

So faith comes from hearing, and hearing through the word of Christ.

Romans 10:17, ESV

The book of Job is thought by many to be the earliest of the Old Testament books to be written. Yet even here, at the dawn of man's written expression, we find a basic question common to all mankind. Job asks, "Can you search out the deep things of God?" (Job 11:7, NKJV).

Throughout man's history, he has sought to gain knowledge as a way of understanding mysterious phenomena. Primitive man developed elaborate explanations to describe factors he could neither understand nor control. Through the years, many accepted and indisputable "facts" have been forced to yield to newer evidence.

People want understanding. And for some strange reason, many persist in thinking that a little knowledge about the components can constitute understanding of the whole. It isn't so. We would question the intelligence of anyone who could observe the thundering majesty of Niagara Falls and dismiss it as "just a lot of H_2O." Yet we often do the same thing with our limited knowledge about the component characteristics of God.

How naïve of us to try to reduce God to some formula that will fit within our minds. Any god who can be described "in a nutshell" belongs there. Some years ago a popular phrase was begun, "Happiness is...." The end of the sentence has been everything from "a warm puppy" to "a bottle of Coke." The lesson is clear—happiness can be described and characterized for years without ever providing a total and exclusive definition.

As with happiness, so with love, truth, and God. They are realities of such scope as to defy complete analysis. Especially in religious faith do we succumb to the natural desire to have everything "cut and dried," "pure and simple." Challenge the cut-and dried concepts of God. God is real. He is many things. But He is more than *all* the things we will ever be able to say about Him.

Having discredited the statements of humans' limited knowledge of God, we must now change sides of the coin and defend the same, for our only method of dealing with the unknown is in terms of the known. We must talk about and think of God in human terms if we are to know Him at all. The differentiation that we must learn to make is between statements "about God" and statements "of God." We must comprehend that total understanding of God is outside our capability, since many of His attributes are outside our experience. This is, of course, why we must live by faith in our relationships with God. Our knowledge of God's characteristics will be only a starting point for our understanding of Him. Knowledge is a foundation of faith.

We really do not know a person simply by meeting Him or by analyzing his physical appearance. We truly know a person only after we have been with him long enough to know and understand some of his qualities. When we note a person's accomplishments and philosophy of life, we draw closer to really knowing him. How a person looks is not nearly so important as *who a person is*.

Our question is, "What things do we know about God that enable us to accept the things we do not know?" The Bible reveals many of the attributes of God.

The High Cost of Knowing God

Before we proceed with God's characteristics, we might be wise to recognize the historically high cost of discipleship. Through the ages people have been willing to give their lives for the exciting knowledge of God and His Son, Jesus.

We live in an age of comfortable Christianity. Not many sacrifices are required of those who wear the name of Jesus. In our generation many have equated church attendance, or the lack of it, with true Christianity. We have developed such shallowness in our Christianity that there is little concern when we put Jesus far down on our list of priorities.

The first-century Christians understood well the price of being a disciple of Christ. In Acts we read of the stoning of Stephen. As the stones ricocheted off his body and bruises appeared and the blood flowed, he understood well the price of being a disciple. In Acts 8, we read of the persecution that began in Jerusalem. "And there arose on that day a great persecution against the church in Jerusalem, and they were all scattered throughout the regions of Judea and Samaria" (Acts 8:1, ESV).

During the early years of the church, while under the reign of Nero, persecution grew more severe. Here are some excerpts from a letter written by the subordinate Roman ruler, Pliny, to the Emperor Trajan: "So far this has been my procedure when people were charged before me with being Christians. I have asked the accused themselves if they were Christians; if they said "Yes," I asked them a second and third time, warning them of the penalty; if they persisted I ordered them to be led off to execution. For I had no doubt that, whatever kind of thing it was that they pleaded guilty to, their stubbornness and unyielding obstinacy at any rate deserved to be punished."

In the third century, Eusebius, the great historian, tells of further persecution: "And the spectacle of affairs after these events exceeds all description. Innumerable multitudes were imprisoned in every place, and the dungeons, formerly destined for murderers and the vilest criminals, were then filled with bishops...and deacons...so that there was no room left for those condemned for crime."

Concerning the persecution in Egypt and Thebes: "We ourselves have observed, when on the spot, many crowded together in one day, some suffering decapitation, some the torments of flames; so that the murderous weapon was completely blunted, and having lost its edge, broke to pieces; and the executioners themselves, wearied with slaughter, were obliged to relieve one another. Then, also, we were witnesses to the most admirable ardour of mind, and the truly divine energy of those that believed in the Christ of God. For as soon as the sentence was pronounced against the first, others rushed forward from other parts of the tribunal before the judge, confessing they were Christians, most indifferent to the dreadful and multiform tortures that awaited them, but declaring themselves fully and in the most undaunted manner on the religion which acknowledges only one Supreme God. They received, indeed, the final sentence of death with gladness and exultation, so far as even to sing and send up hymns of praise and thanksgiving, until they breathed their last."

These martyrs paid the ultimate price for their faith. There is little or no sacrifice required of us; that which is required is often shunned or criticized.

The World's Greatest Power

When we become proud of our multi-megaton bombs and our nuclear fusion research, we should wisely recall that God *spoke* our universe into being; not just our world, but everything. "In the beginning, God created the heavens and the earth" (Genesis 1:1, ESV). The stars were flung into the heavens by God's powerful hand. The earth was made by His creative power. Man was molded by God's artful skill.

The creation gives witness to the power by which God has accomplished His creative works. "O Lord God, you have only begun to show your servant your greatness and your mighty hand. For what god is there in heaven or on earth who can do such works and mighty acts as yours?" (Deuteronomy 3:24, ESV). Jesus described the boundlessness of God's power and strength by saying, "With God all things are possible" (Matthew 19:26, ESV).

God is omnipotent. In Genesis the question is asked, "Is anything too hard for the Lord?" (Genesis 18:14, ESV). The question is answered in the book of Job: "I know that you can do all things, and that no purpose of yours can be thwarted" (Job 42:2, ESV).

God is everywhere. He is omnipresent. In Psalms, the singer says that God knows his every action: "You…are acquainted with all my ways" (Psalm 139:3, ESV). Jeremiah puts it this way: "Can a man hide himself in secret places so that I cannot see him? declares the Lord. Do I not fill heaven and earth? declares the Lord" (Jeremiah 23:24, ESV). He is always present, always with us. Life's greatest tragedy is man's desire to escape from God.

God knows everything. He is omniscient. All wisdom and knowledge come from God. Sometimes we think we have found some new fact when we have only uncovered another aspect of God's creation. All facts have been known to God since the beginning. We are only now stumbling onto some of them. The wise learn to respect the power of God. God is in control; we are only inhabitants of His creation.

Understanding the Christian's Essential Characteristics

If we were to find, or try to find, one word to most nearly epitomize God, the one word would have to be *"love,"* for love is the greatest virtue that we humans readily understand. What is love? We habitually misunderstand the meaning of the word. We say that we love something when really we mean that we like it. We use the word so frequently that it has become trite. Then, when we want to use the word *love* for something or someone as noble as God, the word seems inadequate. Paul said, "But God shows his love for us in that while we were still sinners, Christ died for us" (Romans 5:8, ESV). The apostle John puts it in the simplest terms: "God is love" (1 John 4:8, ESV).

The Bible compares God with a good father, a father to whom we can go with every problem, a father who understands and is near to all of us. God loved man when man rejected Him. He loved man when He gave His Son to die on the cross. We cannot escape God's love. It is impossible. His love is higher than the sky and deeper than the ocean. Travel north, south, east, or west—you will still find yourself surrounded by the love of God.

The Grace of God

The word *"grace"* means "unmerited favor." Man, because of his sin, deserves punishment from God. Despite this fact, God's grace has sought, from the very beginning of man's transgression, a way to save him. Even after we became rebels against Him, God's grace still said, "I will forgive you; I will take you back." "For by grace you have been saved through *faith*" (Ephesians 2:8, ESV, italics mine). God demonstrates His love and grace in the story of the prodigal son and in the Old Testament example of Hosea and Gomer, a father who willingly receives back a spitefully rebellious son and a husband who lovingly buys back his adulterous wife. These examples are as close as God can come to explaining His limitless grace in terms we can understand.

The Bible multiples its examples of God's grace. He sought in every way to save Sodom and Gomorrah. He agreed to save those wicked cities if only fifty righteous people could be found in them. When not even ten could be found, He still allowed the righteous who were there to escape. When sin saturated the world and forced God to destroy His creation, Noah, because of his righteousness, "found *grace* in the eyes of the Lord" (Genesis 6:8,

KJV, italics mine). Time and time again the Israelites were given opportunities to return to God. His longsuffering grace seemed always available. In the same way, God's grace is available to us.

Perfect Justice

The Bible teaches that it is impossible for God to lie. God is the embodiment of truth. Because God cannot lie, all of His Word is true. "All Scripture is breathed out by God" (2 Timothy 3:16, ESV). Christ stated in the gospel of John that the "word is truth" (John 17:17, ESV). Because God is gracious, He permitted His Son to come to this earth and die on the cross to save us. He could not simply remove the sin without atonement; His justice had to be met. He had established in the beginning that if man ate of the tree of the knowledge of good and evil, he would die—both spiritually and physically. We followed Adam's example. We all have sinned, and Jesus had to die in our place to satisfy the justice of God.

God could not lie. The only answer to the sin of man was for God's perfect Son to live among us as a man, to undergo temptation as we do, yet without sin, and then to die as the punishment for sin. He conquered death for His people. Those who refuse this gracious substitution sacrifice of God must eventually pay for their own sins.

All who sin and refuse God's justice and grace must bear their own penalties and consequences. It is just.

Jesus Is God

As part of His saving purpose, Jesus came to live on our earth so that we could know what God is really like. Even with the restraints of His humanity, Jesus far surpassed any quality of life that man had ever known. He gave us a demonstration of what God must be like. He was perfect.

At one point, the disciples were quite confused by all of Jesus' talk about the Father. Philip blurted out, "Lord, show us the Father, and it is enough for us" (John 14:8, ESV). Jesus' reply was, "Have I been with you so long, and you still do not know me, Philip? Whoever has seen me has seen the Father" (John 14:9, ESV).

As we learn more about Jesus, we learn more about God. As we become more loving, we understand more about God. Someday we will know our Creator in all of His indescribable glory. Until that day, we must be content with gradually understanding more about His separate characteristics.

To know God is not enough. It is possible to know all about the phenomenon of light and still never receive the beneficial rays of the sun. You can know about electricity and still not utilize it. You can know all *about* God and still never know *Him*. The only way to know God is by experiencing Him and accepting Him as He is described in the Bible. He must be your personal Savior and Lord.

Salvation comes to man from God. It is a function of His power, His love, His justice, and His grace. It is demonstrated and exemplified in the person of Jesus Christ. Even to know all these things is not to contain God. Such knowledge is only the foundation for knowing God. That must be accomplished through faith.

Food For Thought

1. Was Job's question about God in Job 11:7 (KJV) a fair one? Explain your answer.

2. Can we know everything about God? Why?

3. Does total knowledge about something make it other than faith?

4. Knowing God and having true faith often comes at a high price. What are some of those costs?

5. What has your faith cost you?

6. What are some things we can know about God?

7. How does Jesus teach us about God?

8. Is just knowing about God enough to produce faith? Why?

SECURITY
The By-Product of Faith

And we know that for those who love God all things work together for good, for those who are called according to his purpose.

Romans 8:28, ESV

Christians often give lip service to the idea that God will provide for our needs. Yet the values of our culture and the pressure of our own faithlessness often result in greater dependence on *gold* than on God.

Christians like to read the accounts of the children of Israel, and we marvel that they were blind enough to pass up such an offer of financial security. God promised them wealth in return for faith. They followed for a while, but soon went willfully away from God into want and misery. God, meanwhile, repeatedly made promises of care.

In spite of God's promises, the Israelites made a habit of leaving the security of God. They bowed to idols instead of serving Him. Yet, Christians today should be slow to condemn, for we have often followed their example. With full knowledge of the promise of God's sustaining care, we have often jerked our lives back out of God's hands and tried to run them ourselves, usually by bowing down to the things made by men.

In the New Testament, Jesus reaffirmed God's intention to give us the care we need. The Sermon on the Mount doesn't promise that our corn crop will outgrow the others in the valley, but Jesus does promise that in following Him we will have what we need.

> Therefore I tell you, do not be anxious about your life, what you will eat or what you will drink, nor about your body, what you will put on. Is not life more than food, and the body more than clothing? Look at the birds of the air: they neither sow nor reap nor gather into barns, and yet your heavenly Father feeds them. Are you not of more value than they? And which of you by being anxious can add a single hour to his span of life? And why are you anxious about clothing? Consider the lilies of the field, how they grow: they neither toil nor spin, yet I tell you, even Solomon in all his glory was not arrayed like one of these. But if God so clothes the grass of the field, which today is alive and tomorrow is thrown into the oven, will he not much more clothe you, O you of little faith? Therefore do not be anxious, saying, "What shall we eat?" or "What shall we drink?" or "What shall we wear?" For the Gentiles seek after all these things, and your heavenly Father knows that you need them all. But seek first the kingdom of God and his righteousness, and all these things will be added to you. Therefore do not be anxious about tomorrow, for tomorrow will be anxious for itself. Sufficient for the day is its own trouble (Matthew 6:25-34, ESV).

God has always promised to take care of His people. Under the Old Testament dispensation, He again and again miraculously intervened to rescue His people from jeopardy. On one occasion He brought quail and manna from heaven to feed His children. He gave them a pillar of fire by night and a cloud by day to guide them. God has always provided for those who love Him and are seeking to do His will.

The New Testament reaffirms God's providential care of His people. Jesus brings mankind to a more mature understanding of material security. He not only taught, but demonstrated that a man's life consists not in the things he possesses (Luke 12:15). He brought mankind as close as we have ever been to true material security. Ironically, material security is never attained by getting more things. It is only reached by learning not to need so many things so that they lose their hold over us.

God has promised to care for His own, for those who "seek first the kingdom of God and His righteousness" (Matthew 6:33, ESV). Of course, our human nature causes us to not trust God even though He has proven Himself in the past. The children of Israel received the guidance, direction, and deliverance of God. Even then, they began to murmur and complain. They refused to trust God.

Father Knows Best

God as our Father knows what is best for us. If we will let Him, He will provide what is best. It may be poverty or wealth. It may be health or illness. It may be success or failure. It may be life or death. God knows our needs, both physical and spiritual. Sometimes the physical must be restricted for the spiritual to be advanced.

God will take care of us. He has promised us through His Word that all things are working together for our betterment if we truly love Him and are called according to His purpose (Romans 8:28). Trust is absolutely essential in our relationship with God and with Jesus. Trust is more of an everyday word for the often worn religious term *"faith."* Do you *trust* God? Do you *trust* His power? Do you *trust* His word?

As I began to make a final review of the notes for this chapter, I ran across a very provocative slip of the keyboard. In the process of hastily drafting notes, my transcriber had added an extra letter to the title of a familiar hymn. Only one extra letter, but it changed "God Will Take Care of You" to *"Gold* Will Take Care of You." Perhaps the mistake was not an error! Do we *trust* His promises, or live a life that indicates that our true faith is that "Gold Will Take Care of You?"

Are we willing to put our lives and the lives of our children in the hands of God and trust fully that if we *are* seeking first His kingdom and His righteousness, that God *will* take care of us? Will God take care of us when we contribute even to the point of sacrifice or do we feel a little safer to give a dollar to God and keep the rest for our own needs? Will God take care of us when we walk out on a job for Christian principles, or do we believe that only fanatics are naïve enough not to put the practical necessities of life first? Will God take care of us when we let down our guard and love our neighbors and our enemies, or is it a hard-nosed world that requires stern and harsh retaliation for the offenses of others?

God is the Master of our lives. He knows what is best for our lives. God will take care of us if we are seeking to follow Him. We must not demand a bigger bank balance and better health as proof. Those things may not be what we really need. By turning our lives over to God we will receive exactly what we need and the grace to accept it. It is only after such dependence and trust is in effect that we are able to sincerely pray: "Father...your will be done!" (Matthew 26:42, ESV).

Christ's Concern For Our Bodies

In Matthew there is an incident recorded of Christ healing the blind: "Jesus in pity touched their eyes, and immediately they recovered their sight and followed him" (Matthew 20:34, ESV). In a very real sense, every one of us is spiritually blind. Christ's ability and power to heal the blind of their physical blindness is only an indication of His willingness and ability to heal us of our spiritual blindness and to give us light that we might see and understanding that we might comprehend the abundant life He offers us.

> And he said, "Where have you laid him?" They said to him, "Lord, come and see." Jesus wept. So the Jews said, "See how he loved him!" But some of them said, "Could not he who opened

the eyes of the blind man also have kept this man from dying?" (John 11:34-38, ESV)

Jesus then quickly commanded that the stone be rolled away, and He called for Lazarus to come forth, and he came forth. Again, the power of Christ's conquest over death is an indication that He can give to every one of us spiritual life; we can become new people in Jesus. Christ offers us a spiritual resurrection.

"And when the Lord saw her, he had compassion on her and said to her, 'Do not weep'" (Luke 7:13, ESV). And then He healed her. Jesus is interested in the physical infirmities of mankind today. It is true that He may not work as He once did through individual men to heal others, yet the power of God is still available. In God's own way and according to His own good purpose, He can still heal the physical infirmities of mankind. Even when it is not His will that our bodies should be healed, He can provide for us the strength to bear our infirmities. It was necessary for Paul to continually cope with his infirmity. It may be necessary for our correction and betterment that we too retain a "thorn in the flesh." Christ promises us that He will bring us the strength and power to bear our infirmities.

Christ's Concern For Our Minds

Christ is vitally interested in the mental health of every individual. He wants us to be radiant, happy, and filled with the "peace… which passes all understanding" (Philippians 4:7, ESV). He promises us an abundant life here on this earth if we are willing to love and follow Him. "That evening they brought to him many who were oppressed by demons, and he cast out the spirits with a word and healed all who were sick. This was to fulfill what was spoken by the prophet Isaiah: 'He took our illnesses and bore our diseases'" (Matthew 8:16, 17, ESV). There are many in our troubled world today who need the peace and contentment that can only be found in Jesus. Jesus could say to the woman who was full of guilt as a result of her adulterous life, "Neither do I condemn you; go, and from now on sin no more" (John 8:11, ESV). This woman, no doubt, received great comfort and consolation from understanding fully that she had truly been forgiven. Jesus could tell the woman at the well, "Whoever drinks of the water that I will give him will never thirst again" (John 4:14, ESV). Jesus can add the dimension of completeness to our lives. He can satisfy our every need and fulfill our every longing. In the teachings of Jesus are truths that can bring peace and happiness to each of us. Jesus wants to forgive us and grant us a priceless peace and invaluable hope.

Christ's Concern For Our Souls

When Christians read of the victories and defeats by which God has cared for His people, we look out on a world of suffering. We see mankind lost without hope. We see him blindly searching for a life that is worth the effort. We see him trapped, plagued by the eternal consequences of sin. We see him helpless, hopeless, lost. Then, we see God send His Son to live among men to show the way. We see Jesus dying on a cross for our sins and we know God will take care of us. We see Jesus providing the lost with a way to life. We see Him giving mankind a map in the Bible. We see Him leaving His Spirit to indwell every Christian...and we know God will take care of us. We know that no burden is too heavy, no task too difficult, no journey too long, that God will not take care of us. Amen.

Food For Thought

1. How firm do you believe God can and will meet all your needs?

2. What promises has God made to people of faith?

3. What are some Old Testament examples of God's promises?

4. What are some New Testament examples?

5. What are some ways God takes care of us?

6. In what three areas of our lives did Jesus demonstrate compassion?

7. Give examples of how Jesus cares for us.

8. What is our greatest need?

CHANGE
The Result of Faith

For I am not ashamed of the gospel, for it is the power of God for salvation to everyone who believes, to the Jew first and also to the Greek. For in it the righteousness of God is revealed from faith for faith, as it is written, "The righteous shall live by faith."

Romans 1:16-17, ESV

If we should select one word to describe our generation, it could well be the word *"change."* In almost every area of life, there has been a continual succession and change. There seems to be inborn in man a restlessness and discontentment with things as they are. There is also the logical argument that almost everything can be improved. We are generally favorable to change as a concept; it's only when a specific change happens to step on our toes that we begin to resist "progress." Change is neither good nor bad. It was change that provided the wheel for man's ambition, but it was also change that put the Nazi hate machine in control of a large part of the world. One thing is certain: Change happens as a result of faith. Inventors take a lot of kidding but they persevere because they believe in what they are trying to do. In the world or in our relationships to God, change happens because of faith.

Faith In a Better Way

Man lives in a world of ease and convenience because of our

predecessors' faith in a better way. Changes came by faith and made life much easier for many of us. One hundred and fifty years ago, neither the car nor the airplane had been invented. Today we can hardly imagine a world without these necessities.

American astronauts have traveled 240,000 miles across space to the surface of the moon. Spaceships are the modern wonder of our world. We marvel as we watch those gigantic spears rumbling off the launch pad. We watch them streak through the sky at unbelievable speed and wonder what will come next.

Electricity is a shockingly recent invention. Your great-grandparents lived largely without it, but can you? It lights our homes, powers our computers, TV sets, stoves, and refrigerators. Modern men even put power in little packages to take our conveniences with us. We turn on our radios and hear the voices of people thousands of miles away. We now yawn while watching live color TV from the other side of the world by communications satellite. It is a wonderful, unique generation we live in and it came about through changes—by faith.

Think of the changes resulting from the combustion engine. And what is more passe today than the internal combustion engine? Most engineers now agree that the combustion engine is outdated. If the past is any indicator, we are probably going to power the next generation's activity with some phenomenon yet to be discovered. All this change is certain because faith is acting on men who are acting on faith.

Faith-Progress

Man has made great progress in the field of medicine. Even in the brief history of our country, doctors routinely "bled" people, trying to rid them of infection. George Washington died from such an attempt, yet we can hardly comprehend such a barbaric practice. Needless to say, our descendants will stand aghast at some of our current medical methods. The situation will change because medical researchers have faith.

Inoculations and immunizations have freed us of the fear of smallpox, measles, mumps, and polio. Soon to go are other diseases. Surgery helps thousands of people who would have been "hopeless" cases a few years ago. Many different therapies are being used to successfully treat cancer. Hearts, lungs, livers, and kidneys have all been transplanted from one person's body to another. It is truly an amazing age we live in and it will become even more so—simply because of faith.

Changes in Morality

Not all the changes in our generation have been good ones, however. The moral structure of our nation appears to be weakening daily. At first, in the early history of our country, there was a dedication to moral strength on the part of the majority. Immorality was still a shame in those days. There followed the era of the double standard. It was a time of *private* permissiveness and *public* morality. Then emerged an open permissiveness where people's lives, moral or immoral, were open books for everyone to read. Lately, we have gone a step beyond this: We have come to a period when many are calling bad, good.

The modern morality is not just the old immorality made public. It is a way of assuming anything is all right as long as we talk about it openly. This kind of morality, in effect, says that what has been called sinful or bad in the past is really good. Thus, many who would advocate permissive sex and situation ethics would say that right and wrong are completely relative to the situation and not absolute. These changes have not been good. Their true color is shown by their results. They have brought a chaotic condition to our nation. It *is* good to escape the hypocrisy of the past. But we must also be opposed to ignorant and harmful permissiveness in the present.

Changes in Religion

Many books have been written about the processes of human change. Interestingly enough, the human resistance to change itself seems to be changing. We can delve extensively into the phenomenon, trying to discover the causes and influences of change. In the final analysis, however, we waste our time unless we zero in on the concrete questions of change. Where are we? Where are we going? What changes will get us there? What factors will bring about those changes?

This is especially true concerning the changes in religion. Any casual observer will see that there have been many changes to religion in our time. Many of these changes are not good. It is our generation that has rekindled the doubt in the absolute infallibility of God's Word. It is this generation that has fostered the philosophy of humanism, elevating man and downgrading God. It is this generation that has produced a kind of Christian atheism. Never before would we allow religious leaders to wear the name of Jesus, yet openly preach and practice the concepts of non-believers.

There is a continuing attempt in our world to unite all Christians into one super church. Again, the intention may be good, but the basis of "unity for unity's sake" is bad. The only basis for true and lasting unity is God's Word, the Bible.

In a world of change there are some things that do not change. God does not change. He is not dead nor has He grown old and feeble. He is still powerful, "from everlasting to everlasting" (Psalm 90:2, RSV).

The Bible has not changed either. It was "once for all delivered to the saints" (Jude 3, ESV). It is man's infallible guidebook in every generation.

Man has not changed. He still has the same wants, needs, and desires he has always had. He is still besieged by the same problems. He still fights wars, lies, steals, is immoral, and is continually searching for answers to life's riddles.

It is most comforting to know that Christ also has not changed. Scripture tells us, "Jesus Christ is the same yesterday and today and forever" (Hebrews 13:8, ESV). Jesus Christ is the stabilizing factor in an unstable world. He is an unchanging center of a changing society.

The Turning Point

In the Gospel of Mark, we are given an insight into the dramatic decision point that each person faces at some time in life. It is as though we stand at a fork in the road. We cannot go in both directions, and all eternity hangs upon the choice we make at that turning point.

There once were two young men of approximately the same age, probably thirty to thirty-two. Both were religious leaders; one the leader of an extremist group, a young man who claimed to be the Son of God, the other, though a young man, already a ruler in his religion. One of the young men was rich, the other owned only what He wore. The rich young ruler bowed before Jesus and called Him "good teacher." Jesus told him to stand and gave the glory to God, saying, "No one is good except God alone" (Mark 10:18). The rich young man then asked what he should do to inherit eternal life. Jesus said, "You know the commandments." The ruler then replied that he had kept all of the commandments since his youth. The Scriptures say that Jesus loved him. We are not sure how He expressed this love, perhaps by the compassion in His eyes or in the tone of His voice. But Jesus loved him, as He loves all people.

Jesus said to the young ruler, "One thing you still lack. Sell all that you have and distribute to the poor..." (Luke 18:22, ESV). Many people feel that what Jesus taught was radical. On another occasion He said that if anything stands between you and God, then get rid of it (Matthew 5:29, 30).

Yes, Jesus was a revolutionary. He taught that service to God was most important. Christians are confronted with this same Jesus, and we must decide as did this young ruler whether we will follow Him. If we do choose to allow Him to lead us, then He will make some changes in our lives, possibly even revolutionary changes.

We may be allowing one thing to stand in the way of following Jesus as did this young man. It may be money, as it was with him. Materialism keeps many people from Jesus. It may be relatives, or friends, or pride, or hypocrisy in the church, or a lack of knowledge.

Jesus' people today are living in an age when it is difficult to be a Christian. In fact, many are not even sure who or what a Christian is. Through radio, television, movies, the Internet, and magazines, we are so continually bombarded by sadism, sex, and crime that with too many people, these sins have become expected and accepted.

There are some who are even questioning the possibility of living a Christian life in our time. The Christian life has never been an easy one. It was never described as simple. The Christian life has always required courage, conviction, faith, and sacrifice.

It is often difficult to tell the Christian from the bad guys. The Christian and the non-Christian too many times look alike, dress alike, go to the same places, use the same language. Many enjoy the social benefits and prestige that the name Christian affords, but some are unwilling to pay the price of the discipleship.

Choose Carefully

Every change comes about because of faith in something. If one bases his life-change on greed, selfishness, or pride, he will change into the kind of person the world can well do without. Giving Jesus a place in the motivation of a life-change will produce the good things we already see in Him and His people.

There is also a popular misconception by some that those

who are converted later in life have a deeper appreciation and understanding of what they believe. The theory is that they have already "tried everything" and found that nothing satisfies like Christianity. While the elder brother sits at home, the heroic prodigal is sure of his values, and he is no longer tempted to return to the scene of the prodigality.

It makes an interesting theory. However, the obvious fact is that the devil is too good at his job to ever allow anyone to escape his temptations. He uses whatever is tempting to each person. If one grows up in the church, he may use the sins that were never tried to nag at us and grow ever more appealing. If we didn't escape his early clutches, he is wise enough to use either the pride of our goodness or the time-softening of bitter memories. Regardless of how we have grown up, the enemy of God's people will always find the best way to use that childhood to tempt us.

Actually, faith has to come to each one in pretty much the same fashion. We come to faith by a struggle. We find it when we have to have it—when we want it more than anyone else. The human search for faith is beautifully capsuled in Jesus' statement on the mount: "Blessed are those who hunger and thirst for righteousness, for they shall be satisfied" (Matthew 5:6, ESV). Outward appearances *do* certainly indicate that some folks just slide thoughtlessly into their faith, but the very nature of faith itself forbids this ever happening. Faith is something a person must hammer out for himself. It cannot be inherited. As each generation has discovered, God has no grandchildren.

Regardless of their childhood experiences, God's people have each struggled to establish a personal, meaningful faith. In some cases, the struggle may not appear to be disruptive simply because of the preparation of a religious childhood. Of course, we must not overlook the fact that the church always has had and always will have an abundance of individuals who say "Lord, Lord" and have no faith in Him. We can rest assured, however, that among those whom God counts as His children, each person's faith is one hundred percent personal and meaningful.

Even a person "born in the church" must fight out his system of belief. He may be taken to church regularly. He may memorize the Scriptures before he understands them. He may know all the Bible stories before he has the life experiences to appreciate them. But somewhere, sometime, the relationship of Jesus to real life must be worked out on a one-to-one basis between that individual and God.

It is popular to hold Paul up as an example of the late convert who really, demonstrably changed direction when he was converted. The power of Paul's proclamation is used to demonstrate what good Christians can be made out of folks who are evil. It's a fairly clumsy illustration because Paul probably comes closer to proving the other point of view. His upbringing had been in the strictest "church" teaching available to young Jewish boys. His understanding of the Old Testament Scriptures gave immediate and long-lasting impact to his preaching and writing.

Paul was not great just because of his boyhood training or just because he was killing Christians when he had his faith experience and was ready to turn himself completely over to Jesus. Jesus made Paul great. Jesus can use whatever background we bring to Him. He's not checking spiritual resumes or outward appearances. He works with the hearts of His people.

One Pilgrim's Progress

My own struggle for a deep, personal relationship with the Lord began in my early days of college. I had never questioned the faith that I had been born into until I entered college. I attended a Christian college and was surrounded by Christian peers and had Christian professors. Possibly, this environment gave me an overdose of a good thing. I began to question it all.

My doubt and questioning led me to seek the advice of several men for whom I had the greatest respect and admiration. It also drove me to a desperate personal study of the Bible. I studied that Book in a way I had never studied it before. I suddenly had a different perspective, a different point of view, and a thousand new questions. Now I was reading critically, asking questions, searching for answers.

The struggle intensified after I graduated from David Lipscomb College, a truly outstanding church-affiliated university, and enrolled in the Graduate School of Middle Tennessee State University. It was at MTSU, in a graduate-level philosophy class, that my struggle for faith really came "down to the wire." Day after day, an atheistic professor ridiculed Jesus, the Bible, and the entire Christian faith. He teased that God was old, decrepit, and needed to be retired. He characterized religion as a crutch for barbaric, uncivilized man and maintained that modern, emancipated, sophisticated man no longer needs a crutch called "God."

Each day I would leave the classroom confused, baffled, and uncertain of where to turn. I would struggle through books, commentaries, and magazine articles looking for answers. As I look back I see that my professor was savvy enough to ask questions that had no immediate answers. One of the first lessons I had to learn was patience. The fact that I did not have an answer at that particular moment did not mean that there was no answer. This, for me, was a significant discovery. Often, since that time, I have counseled with people in the midst of a struggle for faith. In almost every case, their first need was for patience. They needed to accept the fact that valuable things take time. Spiritual answers take time in coming.

Many of these dilemmas have now been answered. Those questions for which I thought had no answers now have simple, yet profound answers. It was during that experience that I literally studied for my spiritual life. During my undergraduate days I had searched for a deeper faith because I suspected that the faith I had was not as active and meaningful as it should have been. But during those days of graduate school, my spiritual life was on the line. I was exercising and challenging my faith with some of the toughest philosophical and scientific questions men could ask. I learned from that experience that *more people lose their faith by failing to exercise it than by challenging it.*

In my quest for deeper faith, I searched through many volumes—the Bible, dictionaries, commentaries, books on spiritual renewal. Of all these valuable sources, the greatest satisfaction came from a simple study of the Bible itself. I am convinced that when we return to the source of faith, we will always find the satisfying water which Jesus promised. "Whoever drinks of the water that I will give him will never be thirsty again" (John 4:14, ESV).

I would not be so naïve as to tell you that every one of my questions now have simple answers, but most of them have, and new answers are coming regularly. Certainly, there is more than enough evidence to substantiate the existence and purpose of God, Christ, the Bible, and the church. Don't be ashamed of your doubts. Go to where the answers are. Get into God's Word. "Do your best to present yourself to God as one approved, a worker who has no need to be ashamed, rightly handling the word of truth" (2 Timothy 2:15, ESV).

Faith and Our Security Blankets

During the past few years, I have observed several young people bidding farewell to their faith. These were highly talented and well-educated young men and women. They were delightful to be around. Some were raised in Christian homes and taught Christian principles and doctrines. Most of them attended Christian colleges. Today, they are struggling for faith. The causes of their dilemma are numerous and interwoven. However, some factors emerge as significant.

After marriage, many of these young people immediately moved to large metropolitan areas. If you have ever visited the heart of Manhattan or any big city, you know how lonely one can be, even shoulder-to-shoulder with millions of people. These young people found themselves without any of their familiar religious security blankets. There were no parents to answer questions. Sadly, even when parents are there, they don't always have the right answers. There were no uncles or aunts to look to for guidance and encouragement. They had very few friends. The few friends they *did* have were themselves in the same uncertainty. There was no strong church nearby. The umbilical cord was severed. No family, few friends, weak church, and eventually, little faith.

You need not move to the middle of a big city to experience these types of devastating breaks with security, tradition, and faith. Though having your family nearby can provide subconscious psychological barriers to keep you in the faith, this may be an artificial stimulus for your life and faith. Nevertheless, it can keep you going until you build your own faith. Certainly, when you are an active member of a strong church, you have an advantage in building faith.

One can win the struggle of faith, but there must be a strong desire to do so. One's first step must be a step toward Jesus.

Food For Thought

1. What changes occur when we demonstrate faith in everyday life?

2. What are some examples of good changes brought about by faith?

3. What are some bad results of change?

4. Are there things that should not change? If so, discuss them.

5. What are some changes we may need to make?

6. What bad changes are making it hard for Christians today?

7. Do all good changes come about by faith? Explain.

8. What are some ways our faith begins?

TRIBULATION
The Proof of Faith

Therefore, having been justified by faith, we have peace
with God through our Lord Jesus Christ, through whom
also we have access by faith into this grace in which we
stand, and rejoice in hope of the glory of God.

Romans 5:1-2, NKJV

P eople are constantly asking for honesty. We want people
to simply *be* what they say they are. We are tired of guarantees
that fade and promises that never come true. In the marketplace,
the voting booth, and even the church pew, people are now
demanding accountability.

For years, the classic excuse of those who didn't want to go
to church has been that there are so many hypocrites in the
church. Of course, the person who says this still gets on the
freeway with a lot of daredevils who claim to be drivers, and the
large percentage of duffers can hardly force one to abandon the
golf course. It's an excuse! It is unfortunate to see anyone who
shirks his responsibility because everyone else is going wrong.
Yet, we have to have some sympathy for the folks who have had
an overdose of preaching that doesn't practice and faith that
doesn't fly.

Jesus often had to criticize His followers about their faith.
However, it is interesting and encouraging to note that He didn't
condemn them just for the smallness of their faith, but mostly

for the hypocrisy of it. Jesus' greatest anger and sharpest words of condemnation were directed at the Pharisees for intentionally appearing to have faith when they obviously did not. Because Jesus emphasized the heart of man instead of the outward appearance, He was provoked when He saw people lying to themselves and others about their faith.

If we take the time to sit down and think about it, lying to others is one of the silliest things we do. We have nothing to gain and everything to lose, including the selfrespect that is so difficult to reclaim. God knows the exact condition of our hearts. It is so foolish for us to attempt to lie to God, yet how routinely we lie about our faith when we talk to God in prayer. In the thoughtless hurry of day-to-day living, we rarely take the time to evaluate the faith we claim. When things are going well, talk is cheap and we can speak eloquently about the way we trust God and receive so many blessings from Him.

Fortunately, life is not made up of one hundred percent good fortune. The bad times are mixed with the good; tribulations come to all of us in different measures and to accomplish different purposes. In one sense, our faith is hardly worth sharing until it has stood the test of tribulation.

Imagine a small town that has its first fire engine. Everyone in town passes the fire station and points proudly at the bright, shiny engine. They are happy to have the wonderful new piece of equipment. But if the pump quits and the wheels fall off at the first fire, the people's collective attitude will change. Hopefully, the new fire engine will prove itself when the challenge comes. Then it will rightfully have the confidence and praise of the townspeople. Its tribulation will have proven it to be exactly what its outward appearance has claimed all along.

The more Godlike we become—that is, the more we are able to see things through the perspective of God—the less trauma we experience when life's difficulties come to us. Once we understand that *tribulation comes to polish and prove our faith*, the burdens become somewhat easier to bear. We are able to compare, as Peter did, the tribulations to the fire which burns away the impurities from valuable gold (1 Peter 1:6, 7). Persecutions and adversities often cut away the dead wood and "faith talkers" in the church. When the persecution is over and the smoke clears, the church remains a stronger body, stripped of the hangers-on.

None of us make it a habit to pray for persecution against the church or hard times for ourselves. Yet we know that when God chooses to allow such outward catastrophes to fall upon us, He does so with divine wisdom. He knows we are capable of surviving the tribulation as more useful servants than ever before. If we fall to the trials, it will be because our faith was not at all what we claimed it was.

Suffering can serve either to bring a Christian closer to God, or to lead him further away. It depends on the attitude a Christian has toward suffering. One can take suffering, sorrow, and pain and use it until it becomes a blessing, or one can become embittered, resentful, and cynical and be led further away from God.

All Things?

One of the most commonly quoted Bible verses is Romans 8:28, "And we know that for those who love God all things work together for good, for those who are called according to his purpose" (ESV). No wonder it is such a popular verse for us to use when visiting the sick and distressed. It promises that all bad things which fill the present and all the fears that loom on the horizon are somehow not bad, but good.

We may use Romans 8:28 rather smugly as we try to comfort others in the midst of their tragedies. The real test is not how softly we can whisper this passage. The litmus test is whether or not we think of God and His will at *all* when the knife of human events falls upon us. When Job began to suffer his great physical and emotional tribulations, three of his friends appeared on the scene. They proceeded to debate Job's case and present advice as though Job were a textbook case in a philosophy course instead of a human being in pain. The end result of Job's tribulation is the exposing of the truth about several faiths. Job's own faith emerged victorious and deserving of all the accolades God had given it. Job's friends, on the other hand, had the true colors of their faith exposed. Their faith was in themselves and in their own reasoning. They only *talked about* God.

By the same token, we perhaps should be less presumptuous in our statements about God and His intentions. We so carelessly tell people that we "sympathize" with them, yet like Job's visitors, we are not in their position, not suffering, not bearing the same burden. Also, if we sincerely believe that all things work together for the good of God's people, how can we wish someone to escape a current tribulation? It is perhaps the very thing that God knows he or she needs.

The greater our faith in God and in His divine guidance for our lives, the less able we are to make presumptuous demands upon God in our prayers. We are left with a dependence on God's will. Our prayer changes from, "God, make me well," to "Father, I don't like being sick, but I know that my life is in your hands and that you will do whatever is best for me. I pray your will be done."

All things *do* work together for the good of God's people, but not all of us are godly enough to see the good in all things. We are limited by time and space and perspective. God can see what comes after the tragedy, after death, or around the corner. He knows best, if we will only have faith and submit. An ancient legend tells of an early Christian whose daughter was quite sick. The man begged God strongly that the little girl's life be spared. Later, the girl suffered a terrible death before her father's eyes. The father lamented taking the matter out of God's wise judgment and putting it in his own short-sighted control.

For all our talk about heaven and eternity, we act as if all has been lost when a loved one dies. The early Christians astounded their peers by celebrating when a Christian died; it was no tragedy to them. Their loved one had merely gone to be with God and was, in fact, far better off than they. The difference in people who do not fear death and those who do is *faith*. Death is the ultimate tragedy on the human level. But for the Christian, it is merely another of life's rough spots to grind a polished surface onto one's faith.

So be truly glad! There is wonderful joy ahead, even though the going is rough for a while down here. There trials are only to test your faith, to see whether or not it is strong and pure. It is being tested as fire tests gold and purifies it—and your faith is far more precious to God than mere gold; so if your faith remains strong after being tried in the test tube of fiery trials, it will bring you much praise and glory and honor on the day of his return. (1 Peter 1:6, 7, TLB)

Food For Thought

1. What role does faith play in insulating us from problems?

2. What was Jesus' major criticism of His followers' faith?

3. Why do we often lie about our faith?

4. How should we react to tribulations and sufferings?

5. Does our suffering mean we are doing something wrong?

6. How do all things work for the Christian's good?

7. How should we view the death of a faithful Christian?

8. Comment on 1 Peter 1:6-7 (TLB).

WHO AM I?
The Question of Faith

Now in a great house there are not only vessels of gold and silver but also of wood and clay, some for honorable use, some for dishonorable. Therefore, if anyone cleanses himself from what is dishonorable, he will be a vessel for honorable use, set apart as holy, useful to the master of the house, ready for every good work. So flee youthful passions and pursue righteousness, faith, love, and peace, along with those who call on the Lord from a pure heart.

2 Timothy 2:20-22, ESV

Those of us who are under the control of life's events often enjoy poking fun at the more thoughtful members of our society. We try to prove our rightness by pointing to the mistakes of the mystics and the oversights of the preoccupied. It is our own fears that cause this defensive behavior. It is natural for human beings to wonder about the circumstances of their lives.

In every age, honest and thoughtful people have wanted to know, "Who am I and what is my purpose for living? Why am I here and what am I supposed to accomplish?"

The shallow values and rapid pace of our day make those age-old questions recur with increasing impact. The answers to life's riddles have never come easily, but the misplaced emphasis of our era makes it even harder to get a handle on life—where we come from, where we are going, and why. Each day's newspapers carry fresh accounts of suicides by those who couldn't see any meaning in their lives.

We need to realize that the material world in which we live affords the poorest possible arena in which to think through the values of a life with meaning. The perceived main pursuits of life are food and shelter and the hoarding of things we don't need. How can we sort out our lives if we are constantly distracted by these fringe benefits of real living?

Many young people are confused about life and its values. Perhaps we are more eager to see them eat well and dress sharply than we are to really *know* them. Few would deny that America's teenagers today are better educated and informed than any young people in the past. They know more facts, but there are infinitely more facts to know. The question is whether parents can cope with life better in our skyscrapers than we used to out behind the barn!

Most of the world's present knowledge has been acquired in the last 60 years. Yet with all of this acquisition of knowledge, we are not finding the security and peace we seek. Our high school students today know more than the most learned scientists in the days of Galileo. Yet, though their heads are filled with facts, their hearts are often empty and searching. One of the major questions that haunts them is, "What is the purpose of all of our information and knowledge? To what end are we to use the affluence of this twenty-first century world?"

We are not stupid, just side-tracked. We sense our predicament, and we don't like it. We know that we have all kinds of *information* but little *wisdom*. More and more, groups in our society are dropping out or joining together in the hope of finding the meaning of life. They commune and read and discuss and go around in circles trying to arrive by brute intellectual force at the simple explanations of life that God revealed in the Bible thousands of years ago.

"Who am I and what is the purpose of my existence?" As might be expected, whenever there are questions, there are always plenty of answers. It seems as if the world is always coming up with one more "ism" to keep folks involved so they won't accept the simple, straightforward lifestyle of God.

Fatalism and Pessimism

Socrates said, "Know thyself." Despite the fact that we have advanced in many ways during the intervening years, the man on the street today knows little more about himself than did the average man in Socrates' day. In recent years we have been concentrating on the "easy" directions of advancement, space and technology. Now we must begin to turn our thoughts inward to the really tough work. Having made great strides in conquering outer space, we must awaken to the necessary conquest of inner space—the heart, soul, and mind of man.

The result of many people's inner inventory often seems to be a conclusion of fatalism and pessimism. Writers depict the pessimism of our time. Some have assumed that there is no answer to man's dilemma. Dr. Fred H. Klooster gives this analysis: "True, man has come to a more realistic awareness of himself, but his experience merely shattered his old myths and has left him in skepticism and despair. Violent world wars have shattered the liberal myth of man's innate goodness."

Even if there were no God, pessimism would be a lousy way to live. As the saying goes, an optimist is probably wrong as many times as a pessimist, but he has a lot more fun.

Socialism and Materialism

The Communists have tried for many years to answer the question of the purpose for man. They seek to answer the question through stark materialism, saying that man consists only of chemical elements, that he has a material body and mind, but that there is no such thing as a soul. Most submit that man came into being by some quirk of nature and that he has happened upon his present state by means of evolution.

Communists define God in this way: "The first lie is God...the second lie is right...and when you have freed your mind from the fear of God and childish respect for the fiction of right, then the only remaining chains which bind you are called civilization, property, marriage, morality and justice...they will snap like threads. Let your own happiness be your only law...Our first work must be destruction and annihilation of everything as it now exists. You must accustom yourself to destroy everything, the good along with the bad."

To the materialist, man is simply a tool-using, elevated animal. According to some materialistic theory, the world was formed when a cloud of cosmic dust solidified and became our planet. Through eons of time, life began to develop accidentally. First came the tiny, one-celled amoeba. Eventually, animal life as we know it appeared. A materialist would agree that man is different from the animal world in degree of evolvement but not in kind.

Materialistic socialism teaches that economics controls everything. Their god is the state and the advancement of the state. To have and maintain economic control is the only real purpose of existence. Since there are no spiritual values, the material world is the only world. Therefore, it becomes central. Things become more important than people. Secular socialism stresses the need for and the usefulness of class strife and struggle. Lenin said, "To practice trickery, to employ cunning, to resort to illegitimate methods, and to control the truth is necessary to advance the cause of World Communism."

Communism as practiced today presents a system of non-ethics. Morals are considered altogether relative—changeable according to the goals of the party. Teaching against lying, stealing, murder, and other enemies of human dignity are considered unimportant. Honesty, integrity, and ethics for the Communist must be determined by the situation. Whatever serves the cause of Communism is right.

Communists have little respect for man, the creature. They cannot afford to value the individual, except as a component of a group or class. Since 1917 the Communists have killed more than forty million people, who, in one way or another, stood in opposition to the Communist way. Communists are not interested in individuals—all individuals are dispensable. Only the advancement of the party and the cause is of consequence.

Communism and socialism have no real answer to the question, "Who am I?" Rather, it is the philosophy of those who have decided to pretend that there is no question. But the answer must be found for a question that is so ingrained in man's nature.

Humanism and Hedonism

The humanists of our day tell us that man is only a creature evolved to his present state by organic evolution, possessing no soul and having no eternal destiny. A humanist feels that man's only purpose in existing is the elevation of man himself. To the humanist, the supreme goal of life is to live as long as possible and to improve the condition of mankind physically, mentally, socially, and emotionally. Humanists maintain that all of our effort should be spent in conquering diseases, working out the best system of government and abolishing social evils, such as prejudice and slavery. In effect, let's build our Utopia here.

A hedonist is a humanist who thinks we won't solve these problems, so we might as well lavish on ourselves whatever luxuries, pleasures, comforts, gadgets, and trinkets that would make life more enjoyable. The hedonists are saying, "Let's build a great society and forget all the poverty, hunger, disease, and heartache of the world." Many Christians are practicing hedonists and don't realize it. They are ignoring, like the hedonists, the real needs of mankind. No matter how strongly one believes and practices the "eat, drink, and be merry" Epicurean philosophy, a vacuum remains—an emptiness and an unanswered question, "Who am I, eternally?"

Why Am I Here?

All of us, either consciously or unconsciously, are involved in a great quest, a quest to establish our identity, a quest to find where we have come from, why we are here, and where we are going. These great questions have puzzled man since the beginning of history and they must be adequately answered before man can achieve real faith and purpose in life.

Philosophers, ancient and modern, have tried to answer many of the riddles of life, but when it comes to this one—the purpose of man's existence, the why for our being on earth—they are left with no answer. Renan, the French philosopher and skeptic, said, "We are living on the perfume of an empty vase." Nietzsche, the German philosopher, wrote, "Where is my home? For it do I seek and have sought, but have not found it. Oh, eternal everywhere, oh, eternal nowhere, oh, eternal in vain." The 19th century American infidel Robert Ingersoll said, "Life is a narrow vale between the cold and bare peaks of two eternities. We strive in vain to look beyond the heights. We cry aloud and the only answer is the echo of our wailing cry." Bertrand Russell stated, "The life of man is a long search through the night, surrounded by invisible foes, tortured by weariness and pain, toward the goal which few can hope to reach and where none can tarry long."

Mark Twain, who is known for his ability to make people laugh, was a lonely and skeptical man inside. His view of man's purpose is empty: "A myriad of men are born. They labor and sweat and struggle for bread. They squabble and scold and fight. They scramble for little-meaning advantages over each other. Age creeps upon them, infirmities follow, shame and humiliation brings down their pride and their vanity. Those they love are taken from them and the joys of life are turned into aching grief. The burden of pain, care, and misery grows heavier year by year. At length ambition is dead, pride is dead, vanity is dead; longing for relief is in their place. It comes at last, the only unpoisoned gift earth ever had for them, and they vanish from a world where they were of no consequence, where they achieved nothing, and where they were a mistake, a failure, and a foolishness; where they have left no sign where they existed—a world which will lament for a day and forget them forever. Then another myriad takes their place and copies all they did and goes along the same profitless road and vanishes as they vanished to make room for another million other myriads to follow in that same arid path through the same desert and to accomplish what the first myriad and all the myriads that come after it accomplished—nothing!"

Many philosophers are eloquent when voicing their opposition to Christian faith. Many scoff at Christian principles. But such philosophers and skeptics tend to be an unhappy, purposeless group who have mostly questions and few good answers. Many must have proof of everything, yet they will believe only what they can see. Their lives are cold and empty, without meaning, dismal and unhappy; yet, some would ask us to accept their unhappy philosophy.

In a sense, all of us are philosophers in that we each have a philosophy of life, conscious or unconscious.

God's Answer

God is seeking to answer for us through Jesus the question of why we are here. Jesus came to the earth to bring man back into a right relationship with God, to repair the severed diplomatic relations between each of us and God. He came to serve the purpose of God. "As he is so also are we in this world" (1 John 4:17, ESV). If we can find Christ's reason for being here, then we will have our reason.

Paul tells us, "Have this mind among yourselves, which is yours in Christ Jesus, who, though he was in the form of God, did not count equality with God a thing to be grasped, but emptied himself, by taking the form of a servant, being born in the likeness of men. And being found in human form, he humbled himself by becoming obedient to the point of death, even death on a cross" (Philippians 2:5-8, ESV). Jesus did not look at what life was to cost Him, but rather at what He could give to life. For us to be like Jesus means that we, too, must lay aside claims to self and seek what is best for others and for God's purposes. This, in reality, is what is best for us.

"By this all people will know that you are my disciples, if you have love for one another" (John 13:35, ESV). Jesus has a love for everyone and sees the real worth of every man made in the image of God, and so must we.

Why are we here? God has not *left* us here but has *placed* us here for a purpose— to be witnesses of Himself to the world. Even as Jesus was the revelation of the nature of God to the world, so we must also be the revelation of God in Christ's absence. He left His disciples with the commission, "As the Father has sent me, even so I am sending you" (John 20:21, ESV).

What Happens Next?

God made our world, but He did not make it eternal. He made it to serve His own purpose; when that purpose is served, the world will end. We are living in the last stages of God's purpose for the world. Peter referred to this dispensation as the "last days" (2 Peter 3:3).

Even scientists who do not believe the Bible as the inspired word of God agree that our world is running down and that some day it will end. Several theories are held as to how the world will come to an end. Some believe that a decrease of magnetic attractions will some day throw the earth out of orbit, and the earth will collide with another planet and end in a fiery explosion. Others say that the intense heat and pressure within the center of the earth will cause a gigantic earthquake. Astronomers with high-powered telescopes often see the end of star systems like ours. Some tell us that the running down of the sun will bring about the end of the world by freezing everything on earth. Some even believe that, as a result of a chain reaction from nuclear explosions, the earth will come to a violent end. All of these are only theories; no one knows for sure how the world will come to an end. "But the day of the Lord will come like a thief, and then the heavens will pass away with a roar, and the heavenly bodies will be burned up and dissolved, and the earth and the works that are done on it will be exposed" (2 Peter 3:10, ESV).

The Noble Heritage

The Bible tells us that we are creatures of God. God made us in His own image—man bears the image of God! What an ennobling concept of man's nature—man differs from all other creatures in the world. He belongs to the same order of beings as God Himself.

Because men are made in the likeness of God, we can *know* Him. In the beginning, man and God talked together, but because of wrong decisions, man became separated from God. Man's purpose in life is to get back into his rightful relationship with God.

Only God's Word adequately and completely answers man's question: "Who am I?" The Bible tells us that we are made in the image of God, possessing mind, body, and soul, living here with one purpose: to serve God that we might fulfill our eternal purpose.

Most humans try to know God. The most primitive tribes, the idolworshippers, and the sophisticated city-dwellers are all striving in some way to affirm, "I am God's...I belong to God...I know God." When man realizes the true relationship he has with

God, he is awed. God is so powerful that He speaks and matter takes form, breathes, and lives. We don't have to fully understand it to accept it. When David realized all that God had done in creating the world, he asked the question, "What is man that you are mindful of him, and the son of man that you care for him? Yet you have made him a little lower than the heavenly beings and crowned him with glory and honor" (Psalm 8:4, 5, ESV).

Neither ancient nor modern philosophies have provided the answer to man's great riddle, "Who am I?" Only God can answer that question adequately. Only His answer gives true meaning to life. Nietzsche said, "If a man has a *why* for his life, he can bear almost any how." Albert Camus said, "Here is what frightens men; to see the senses of this life dissipate, to see our reason for existence disappear; that is what is so intolerable. Man cannot live without meaning."

Man made in God's image does have meaning. There is nobility, purpose, destiny, and true meaning to life when we develop faith in Jesus. "Apart from Jesus Christ, we know not what our life is, nor our death, nor God, nor ourselves" wrote Pascal. With Jesus Christ we can *know*...through faith.

Food For Thought

1. How does our material world make it difficult to answer: Where do we come from? Why are we here? Where are we going?

2. How can information help in our quest for faith?

3. Why are so many non-Christian people filled with fatalism and pessimism?

4. Why can materialistic socialism never fill our souls?

5. What do communist, socialists, and materialists all have in common?

6. What is the humanist's main purpose in life?

7. Why are we here?

8. Discuss God's answer for our purpose on earth.

THE BIBLE
Chronicle to Faith

For with the heart one believes unto righteousness, and with the mouth confession is made unto salvation. For the Scripture says, "Whoever believes on Him will not be put to shame." For there is no distinction between Jew and Greek, for the same Lord over all is rich to all who call upon Him. For "whoever calls on the name of the Lord shall be saved."

How then shall they call on Him in whom they have not believed? And how shall they believe in Him of whom they have not heard? And how shall they hear without a preacher? And how shall they preach unless they are sent? As it is written:

"How beautiful are the feet of those who preach the gospel of peace, Who bring glad tidings of good things!"

Romans 10:10-15, NKJV

In every generation there have been some who tried to destroy God's written word. They have usually sought to destroy it by attacking the validity or accuracy of its history, its science, or its archaeology. In every case, the Bible has been proven rather than pulverized. Of course, modern philosophers are still after the book. They are calling the Bible a simplistic fairy tale.

The Supreme Court has banned its reading from our schools, and many Bibles are only used for taking oaths these days. Often, the Bible is only a dust collector, a showpiece, or a storage place. It has little real effect in people's lives. Regular Bible reading gave us several generations of great leaders. Today, most seldom read it.

In ancient times there were rulers who tried to destroy the Bible by mass burnings. Copies of the Scriptures were seized wherever found, placed in a central location in the city, and burned. Occasionally, Christians who refused to reveal the whereabouts of their Scriptures were tossed into the fire as an example to others.

There have been those throughout history who have prophesied the impending end of the Bible. The eighteenth-century French skeptic, Voltaire, said, "In less than a hundred years, the Bible will be discarded and Christianity swept from the earth."

In 1794, Thomas Paine published his *Age of Reason*. Paine unleashed a vicious attack against the Bible. He said that he would go through the Bible like a wood chopped with an axe and that within the century it would die. How many people today read the works of Thomas Paine? The Bible is still the world's best seller!

In 1885 Robert Ingersoll delivered a shocking speech called "The Mistakes of Moses." The noted atheist prophesied that within twenty-five years, there would be no more church buildings erected. Most of our church buildings have been built since that time.

On November 16, 1925, the American Association for the Advancement of Atheism announced that it was declaring war to get rid of religion. Their war has been unsuccessful. Today we could almost wish someone cared enough about the Bible *to* declare war on it.

John Wycliffe was condemned for heresy by the Senate of Oxford in 1383; his crime was translating the Bible. Hitler tried to destroy the Bible and viewed it as his enemy.

All attempts to destroy the Bible have ended in failure. The Bible bears its own testimony in the words of Jesus: "Heaven and earth will pass away, but my words will not pass away" (Mark 13:31, ESV). The book-burning infidels, the pompous skeptics, even the rejection by the masses will never be enough to destroy this book—for it is of God.

Why Some Dislike the Bible

God has promised that by Providence the Bible will remain for every generation (1 Peter 1:25). Countless thousands of men and women through the centuries have died so that the Scriptures might live. There is a reason for God's providence and man's sacrifice in preserving the Scriptures. The reason is that the Bible is man's guidebook while upon the earth.

Why is there so much crime, brutality, immorality, mental illness, and insecurity in our world today? It is because man has drifted so far from God and His Word. He has turned his back on his only possible hope. If only we had eyes in the back of our heads to see the pictures of the past! Without exception, when man has rejected God, he has lost his way.

Ahab, one of the ancient kings of the Old Testament, sought counsel from prophets about a battle that was to take place. He didn't like what the prophet of God said, so he called in other prophets. These were "false" prophets who said what he wanted to hear (1 Kings 22:2-28). So it is with our generation. Many don't like what the Bible says, so they turn to those who will say what they want to hear.

We live in a generation that resists rulers, despises boundaries, and rebels at law. But we must realize that if we live without restrictions, we must reap the rewards of our dog-eat-dog society. "It is not in man who walks to direct his steps" (Jeremiah 10:23, ESV).

It is only in the Bible that the proper boundaries of man's existence are found. Modern, permissive immorality is creating a generation with little pride, few values, and casual concerns. Men, in their desire to be happy, are following the pseudo-philosophers as they lead them further and further from real purpose and happiness.

Many people are seeing the folly of the humanistic philosophies, which strip man of his pride and purpose and leave him with nothing but an empty shell. Only the Bible tells us who we are, where we came from, and where we are going. Even so, many men hate the Bible because it is the light of God, exposing their evil lives (John 3:20).

All Can Study the Bible Today

Many know their morning newspapers better than they know the Bible. There was a time when the Scriptures were chained to the pulpits and only the priests or religious leaders could read them, because they felt that the common people did not have enough intelligence to understand the Bible. Today, we live in an age when the Bible is accessible. Because the Bible is so familiar, it is all too often taken for granted. In ancient times, printing was unknown; each copy of the Scriptures had to be printed by hand, checked and rechecked to make sure there were no errors. With modern printing methods, the Bible is readily available to all of us. But where there is great availability, there is also great responsibility.

Understanding the Bible

When some people begin reading the Bible, they tend to jump to conclusions they would never consider in reading other literature. Some readers will take statements out of context, take the literal figuratively, and the figurative literally. A few simple facts can make Bible reading easier and clearer. The real secret in studying the Bible is to understand the historical divisions of the Bible and the groups to whom each was primarily directed.

The Bible is divided into the Old Testament and the New

Testament. From Adam to Moses extended the Patriarchal period, when God spoke directly to the heads of families; i.e., the patriarchs. The first dispensation, or period, lasted about 2,500 years. It was followed by the Mosaic dispensation, which began with Moses and ended with the death of Christ. This second dispensation lasted about 1,500 years. Today we are living in the Christian dispensation. It will last until the end of time. Hebrews 1:1, 2 tells how God has used various messengers during these different dispensations.

The Old Testament is a schoolmaster to take us to the New Testament (Galatians 3:24). "By canceling the record of debt that stood against us with its legal demands. This he set aside, nailing it to the cross" (Colossians 2:14, ESV). Christ fulfilled the old law by living a perfect life and dying on the cross.

Understanding these important divisions of the Bible keeps us from getting confused about God's instructions regarding how we should worship and live. We no longer burn incense or offer animal sacrifices or worship in the temple on the Sabbath as the Jews did in the Mosaic era. Today, we are under the Christian dispensation. The Old Testament gives us the information we need to understand how the New Testament came about and why it was necessary. There is also some of the Old Testament that is incorporated in the New Testament.

The Only Basis For Unity

The plea for unity is being sounded by many denominations. It seems that our generation is seeking more than anything else one element in religion: unity. Christians who have never questioned religious institutions are now taking a fresh look at our situation. We know there is something desperately wrong with twenty-first century Christianity, but thus far, many have not been able to put a finger on this malignant problem.

The peoples of Asia and the Far East have seen in our Christianity what we in America have not been able to see. Just after World War II, there was a massive move of American missionaries to Japan and other Far East countries. At first there was success as thousands left their ancestor worship and came to Christianity. It wasn't long, however, until the people of the East began to see what we still are not able to see fully. They were able to look objectively at Christianity, not being biased by denomination-alism or their parents' religion. To them, Christianity was only a generation or so old. What they saw caused them to wonder. One missionary would step off the boat, build a building, and put a sign in the church yard advertising his brand of Christianity. Down the road another missionary would set up his church, wearing a different name from that of the first, and teaching a different doctrine. Both claimed to be Christians; both claimed to be worshipping the same God. As the people of the East looked about, they found many different denominations teaching different doctrines, emphasizing varied beliefs. Most of the time, these beliefs contradicted one another. What the people of these nations saw was that twenty-first century Christianity is a religion of division, confusion, contradiction, and often contention. Many of the people of Asia and other parts of the world have rejected Christianity because they believe the confusion they see could not be truth.

Could it be that we need to take a new look at Christianity? Is it possible for us to have truth yet teach doctrines that are totally opposed to one another?

The statement of Jesus that "If a house is divided against itself, that house will not be able to stand" (Mark 3:25, ESV), although referring to the kingdom of Satan, it is being proved true today in regard to Christianity. The world is looking with suspicion on our divided house. What is the hope of our Christian world? It is in the one word—, unity, based on faith in God and His Word.

As G. K. Chesterton stated, it is not that Christianity has been tried and found wanting. It simply has not been truly tried.

Food For Thought

1. Why do some people want to destroy the Bible?

2. Why have men been willing to die to preserve the Bible?

3. Why do people ignore the Bible?

4. What are some principles involved in understanding the Bible?

5. What is our only basis for unity?

6. Is it possible to have truth and teach doctrines that are contradictory to one another?

HEAVEN
The Reward of Faith

"Let not your hearts be troubled. Believe in God; believe also in me. In my Father's house are many rooms. If it were not so, would I have told you that I go to prepare a place for you? And if I go and prepare a place for you, I will come again and will take you to myself, that where I am you may be also. And you know the way to where I am going." Thomas said to him, "Lord, we do not know where you are going. How can we know the way?" Jesus said to him, "I am the way, and the truth, and the life. No one comes to the Father except through me.

John 14:1-6, ESV

A Sunday School teacher teaching a group of five-year-olds asked them, "How many of you would like to go to heaven?" All of the hands in the group went up but one. Little Janet, sitting on the front row, was asked why she didn't want to go to heaven. She explained, "Well, teacher, I'd like to go to heaven, but my mother told me to come straight home after Sunday School."

Heaven is the dream of every Christian. For centuries our poets have spoken of a Utopia, that perfect place where men and women would live in perpetual happiness. But the Bible plainly teaches that this is not our home. The earth is merely a testing ground on which we are tried. Certainly we should be constantly trying to better the world conditions by improving relationships with other nations, by conquering all the diseases we possibly can, but even at best, this earth will never become a heaven. There will always be "wars and rumors of wars" (Matthew 24:6, ESV), and as long as men live there will be sickness, sorrow, and death.

Heaven is the prize at the end of the race run in faith here on earth. Paul said, "I press on toward the goal for the prize of the upward call of God in Christ Jesus" (Philippians 3:14, ESV), and that prize toward which all of us are working is heaven. Being able to spend eternity with God, Christ, and the faithful of all ages is a glorious hope.

Heaven is a real place. There are those who try to tell us that it is an imaginary place, but Christ promised "I go to prepare a place for you" (John 14:2, ESV). Heaven, then, is no figment of anyone's imagination, no fairy tale for overgrown children. It is a real, actual place where the faithful of God spend eternity.

We Will Meet God and Jesus

The longing of every Christian is to meet his Maker and Savior. In heaven we will be able to see God and Jesus face-to-face. I am certain all of us have speculated at one time or another what God and Jesus must really look like, especially, I suppose, what Christ looked like when He was here on earth. But in heaven, we will have no doubt for there we will meet them face-to-face.

In heaven, we will meet those who have gone before. We will be united with the great apostle Paul, with Peter, and all of the faithful of all the ages. Isaac, Jacob, and Abraham will be there, as will Moses and those other faithful of God of the past. Jesus said, "...many will come from east and west and recline at table with Abraham, Isaac and Jacob in the kingdom of heaven" (Matthew 8:11, ESV). These are our spiritual relatives and in one sense, they should be closer than our relatives here on earth. These are our brothers and sisters in Jesus. God is our Father and we are a family. In heaven, there will be a great family reunion of all of God's children of all ages.

Heaven May Mean More to Some Than to Others

Christ, when He was here on earth, spoke to the poor and dejected, those who have little of the earth's goods. Occasionally, He spoke to an influential or rich person, but the masses of His followers were the poor. To a man with nothing to call his own, a wonderful home in heaven has a great attraction, but to a man who has much in this life, who owns a mansion here, the appeal is somewhat lessened. People sometimes wonder whether there will be degrees of reward in heaven. We can only say that it is possible that there will be degrees of appreciation. One of the rules of life is that we get out of anything what we put into it. There are some who put more into their Christianity than others, and as a result, may get more out of heaven.

Some would not be happy in heaven. They had no concern for God here on earth, they certainly don't love Jesus, and they are not seeking to follow Him. They shun Christian association because they feel uncomfortable around Christians. To them, the Bible is just a book like any other book; it has no power in their lives. This kind of person would be uncomfortable in heaven, would not be happy there. There are others here on earth who do the minimum, just barely fulfilling their Christian responsibilities, and then there are those who go the second mile, who do all that is humanly possible to do for Jesus. These people will receive the full joy and bliss of heaven.

Heaven Is Eternal

After a lifetime of devotion to God, He promises us a secure home. Today we have a system of "social security." A person pays into it during the working years of his life, then, when he is older, he can retire with a feeling of security, knowing that his needs are going to be met in his old age. After a person has served God faithfully all his life, has worked hard in His kingdom and for His cause, then God promises a secure eternal existence in Heaven.

"For here we have no lasting city, but we seek the city that is to come" (Hebrews 13:14, ESV). Nations rise and fall, cities are built, abandoned, or destroyed. Today, in part of the ancient world, cities are being excavated that have been buried under rubble for centuries. Truly, we have no continuing city here. In a matter of moments, the ravages of war can destroy a city that has stood for countless generations; but in heaven, we'll live in an eternal city.

It's like the little girl who said she wished she had a peppermint stick with only one end; heaven will be so enjoyable that we will want it to never end. And the wonderful part is, it never will.

Heaven is a Beautiful Place

Here we try to make our homes as beautiful as possible. We choose the most attractive architectural plans, sometimes even hiring an architect to make a custom design. We want the best contractor available to build to our specifications. When building our dream homes, we want them to be as beautiful as our dreams. Heaven is a city "whose designer and builder is God" (Hebrews 11:10, ESV). In heaven, God is the architect and Christ is the contractor. Heaven will be the most beautiful place ever imagined.

In heaven, our home will not be a "shack on the wrong side of the tracks," but a mansion on the finest street. Every home will be a castle. "In my Father's house are many rooms. If it were not so, would I have told you that I go to prepare a place for you? And if I go and prepare a place for you, I will come again and will take you to myself, that where I am you may be also" (John 14:2, 3, ESV). Heaven is not just a stately mansion; it is a home, and provides all of the charm, love, warmth, and goodness that any good Christian home would provide here. Heaven is the home of the soul.

> Then I saw a new heaven and a new earth, for the first heaven and the first earth had passed away, and the sea was no more. And I saw the holy city, new Jerusalem, coming down out of heaven from God, prepared as a bride adorned for her husband.

And I heard a loud voice from the throne saying, "Behold, the dwelling place of God is with man. He will dwell with them, and they will be his people, and God himself will be with them as their God. He will wipe away every tear from their eyes, and death shall be no more, neither shall there be mourning, nor crying, nor pain anymore, for the former things have passed away" (Revelation 21:1-4, ESV).

And he carried me away in the Spirit to a great, high mountain, and showed me the holy city Jerusalem coming down out of heaven from God, having the glory of God, its radiance like a most rare jewel, like a jasper, clear as crystal (Revelation 21:10, 11, ESV).

And the one who spoke with me had a measuring rod of gold to measure the city and its gates and its walls (Revelation 21:15, ESV).

The wall was built of jasper, while the city was pure gold, like clear glass. The foundations of the wall of the city were adorned with every kind of jewel. The first was jasper, the second sapphire, the third agate, the fourth emerald, the fifth onyx, the sixth carnelian, the seventh chrysolite, the eighth beryl, the ninth topaz, the tenth chrysoprase, the eleventh jacinth, the twelfth amethyst. The twelve gates were twelve pearls, each of the gates made of a single pearl, and the street of the city was pure gold, like transparent glass (Revelation 21:18-21, ESV).

And the city has no need of sun or moon to shine on it, for the glory of God gives it light, and its lamp is the Lamb (Revelation 21:23, ESV).

John is saying that heaven is going to be more beautiful than anything we can possibly imagine. The finest of this earth is the only way to describe in some measure the beauty of heaven, but there really is no way we can completely comprehend how marvelous it will be. Even in our most elaborate imaginations, we can't visualize heaven.

Heaven Is a Haven

Heaven is a haven of rest. Rest is essential to health and happiness. Sometimes we feel as if we are abused and persecuted, but Paul said, "I consider that the sufferings of this present time are not worth comparing with the glory that is to be revealed to us" (Romans 8:18, ESV). "For this light momentary affliction is preparing for us an eternal weight of glory beyond all comparison" (2 Corinthians 4:17, ESV). This passage meant a great deal to those in the early church who were sawn asunder, crucified, cast into bears' pits and lions' dens, whose lives were constantly in jeopardy for the cause of Jesus. It means much to us when we are ridiculed, laughed at, called cowards and "chicken"; we need to realize, as Paul said, the sufferings of this present time cannot be compared with the glory to come.

Paul said at the end of his life, "I have fought the good fight, I have finished the race, I have kept the faith. Henceforth there is laid up for me the crown of righteousness, which the Lord, the righteous judge, will award to me on that Day, and not only to me but also to all who have loved his appearing" (2 Timothy 4:7, 8, ESV). At the end of a life of toil and sacrifice, God provides a haven of rest.

Heaven is also a haven from sorrow and death. Here, we cry and mourn, we know each other, love each other, and then must be separated from each other by death, but in heaven, there will be no tears. Here, we shed tears of disappointment; people and events often let us down. People make promises and break them. They claim to be telling the truth and lie to us. Children disappoint parents, parents disappoint children. Employers disappoint their employees. In heaven, there will be no tears of disappointment.

Here, we shed tears over unfulfilled dreams. A person reaches middle age and realizes it's now impossible to fulfill his beautiful dreams, and tears are shed. In heaven, our eternal dreams will come true. Here, we shed tears over the loss of loved ones. This is one of the most painful experiences known to mankind, but in heaven there will be no more death. "He will wipe away every tear from their eyes, and death shall be no more, neither shall there be mourning, nor crying, nor pain anymore, for the former things have passed away" (Revelation 21:4, ESV). Jesus promised His disciples on His last night with them before His death, "Let not your hearts be troubled. Believe in God; believe also in me. In my Father's house are many rooms. If it were not so, would I have told you that I go to prepare a place for you? And if I go and prepare a place for you, I will come again and will take you to myself, that where I am you may be also" (John 14:1-3, ESV). In heaven, God will provide for all of our needs.

Heaven is a prepared place for prepared people. We prepare here for there. Heaven is a place for faithful Christians. There will be no salvation outside of Christ. Only in Christ and through Christ can we ever hope to achieve heaven. But simply being a Christian in name only is not enough; we must be faithful until death. Will you begin your preparation today so that someday heaven will be your home?

Food For Thought

1. Faith has its rewards. What are some of them?

2. Heaven should be our goal. What are some reasons?

3. Why may heaven mean more to some than others?

4. How does the Bible describe heaven?

5. Discuss your feelings about an eternity with no more pain, suffering, sorrow, death.

6. In our faithless world, how do we keep our eye on the prize?

7. Discuss Jesus' words in John 14:1-3.

8. What is most appealing about heaven to you?

TRUE HAPPINESS
A Bonus of Faith

But you, O man of God, flee these things and pursue righteousness, godliness, faith, love, patience, gentleness. I urge you in the sight of God who gives life to all things.

1 Timothy 6:11, 13a, NKJV

I believe that every Christian saved by grace through faith should be happy. John 10:10 states that Jesus came to give us life more abundantly. Why shouldn't Christians be happy? God has forgiven our sins. He promises us peace that passes understanding. We have joy, love, and faith in our lives. Christians should shine like bright stars against the black sky. Jesus said, "You are the light of the world" (Matthew 5:14, ESV).

Not all Christians, though, are happy, nor are they content. Some are glum, negative, and see only the bad and rarely ever the good. Some Christians have little or no joy—why is that? The truth is that happiness is an attitude more than anything else. Happiness is a choice. True happiness or joy is not dependent on health, success, wealth, or any other external thing. Happiness is a result of right thinking.

I knew a man who at the age of 30 was confined to a wheelchair with rheumatoid arthritis. His body was twisted and distorted, but his spirit and mind were as healthy as anyone I've ever known. The purpose of my visit was to cheer him up, but he ended up cheering me. On visiting him numerous times, I never saw him without a smile. His pleasant personality was an inspiration to everyone. Though in physical pain, he always had a joke or funny story. He once confided to me that he believed he was confined to his small home in a wheelchair so that he could help people who needed uplifting and encouragement. Literally hundreds of people yearly would seek his wisdom and counsel. Some of the happiest people I know are not physically well or healthy. "One's life does not consist in the abundance of his possessions" (Luke 12:15, ESV).

Every feeling, attitude, or characteristic of happiness is just as available to the poor as to the rich. Our feelings, character, attitude, and happiness are not dependent on race, gender, money, or health, but rather in how we think—our attitudes and thought patterns. There are poor, sick, rich, educated, and uneducated happy people. All have the possibility of happiness if they think and act correctly to the circumstance of their life. Everyone has the potential to be a happy, content, fulfilled person. Often we think if we only had a little more money, a little better health or education, we would be happy. But why not be happy now? Yes, strive to improve and be better in every area of your life but be happy now. Paul said "I have learned in whatever situation I am to be content" (Philippians 4:11, ESV). Paul continually wanted to improve his life but was content with the circumstances of his life.

Some of the unhappiest people I know are rich, educated, and some are even famous. Conversely, some of the happiest people I know are poor, uneducated, and anonymous. What produces happiness, fulfillment, or success? It is primarily learning to get along with one another and with God. The key to happiness is in right thinking and living. The only way we can know how to live right is by going to the instruction book God gave us, which is His Word—the Bible—and applying the principles and attitudes it offers us.

The first commandment is to love God. This is essential to true completeness and fulfillment. The second commandment is to love our neighbors as we love ourselves. In loving others, we find a fulfillment needed in the human psyche. People like people who like them. True happiness comes from loving others and wanting what is best for them, applying the golden rule: "And just as you want men to do to you, you also do to them likewise" (Luke 6:31, NKJV). Bitterness, hatred, and resentment towards others destroy happiness. People who like to fight are only happy when they win, and sometimes not even then. A bulldog can beat a skunk in a fight, but it is just not worth the effort. True happiness comes from not only loving others but also from wanting to help them, investing some of our time, effort, and energy in making their lives better and happier. Ministering to others is a true talent. Jesus said, "the Son of Man came not to be served, but to serve" (Matthew 20:28, ESV). Being self-centered is the surest way to be unhappy and make others unhappy. What we have been saying runs counter to everything we see and hear today, doesn't it?

Many people have a selfish attitude, wanting everything for themselves and wanting every experience to be about them. This is seeking happiness in a direct, narcissistic way that always ends in unhappiness. Happiness comes indirectly from living the right kind of life and helping others. Jesus' life was one of giving to others and God continually. He was always healing, comforting, teaching, and sharing God's secrets of true happiness—, and His was the most successful and fulfilled life ever lived. Faith should lead us to this philosophy of life: Love God first and our fellow men as ourselves. "For you know the grace of our Lord Jesus Christ, that though he was rich, yet for your sake he became poor, so that you by his poverty might become rich" (2 Corinthians 8:9, ESV). "For we do not have a high priest who is unable to sympathize with our weaknesses, but one who in every respect has been tempted as we are, yet without sin" (Hebrews 4:15, ESV).

If you will study the history of Christ's ministry from baptism to ascension, you will discover that it is mostly made up of little words, little deeds, little prayers, little sympathies, adding themselves together in a weird succession. The Gospel is full of divine attempts to help and to heal in body, mind, and heart, individuals. The complete beauty of Christ's life is only the added beauty of little inconspicuous acts of kindness. Talking with the woman at the well; going far into the north country to talk with the Syro-Phonecian woman; showing the young ruler the stealthy ambitions laid away in his heart that kept him away from the kingdom of heaven; shedding a tear at the grave of Lazarus; teaching a little knot of followers how to pray; teaching the Gospel one Sunday afternoon to two disciples going to Emmaus; kindling a fire and broiling some fish that his disciples might have breakfast waiting on them when they came ashore from a night's fishing, cold, tired, and discouraged. All of these things, you see, lead us so easily to the real qualities and tone of God's interest, so specific, so narrowed, so enlisted in what is small, so engrossed in what is minute.

To feel as others feel, to hurt when others hurt, to weep when others have sorrow and pain, to feel deeply for others and about others, is truly a rare and beautiful quality. Call it compassion, or sympathy, or empathy. Call it what you will, it is needed in the personality of a Christian.

People like to be around others who love and appreciate them. Try this experiment: Be genuinely interested in others. Smile, speak to them, help them, and most of all, listen to them. Don't talk; don't tell your story, just listen to theirs. Be genuinely empathetic. Make little sacrifices of time and effort for them. If you do this, you will have more friends than you ever imagined or dreamed possible. You will be popular and personally happier than you have ever been. Giving of ourselves to others fulfills a basic human need of using our talents, time, money, and energy in a constructive, helpful way.

Another Reason for Happiness

Another reason Christians should be happy is because of the promises of God. Most people of faith believe God's commands and demands, but we should all equally believe His promises and blessings. God promises to provide for all our physical needs.

> Therefore I tell you, do not be anxious about your life, what you will eat or what you will drink, nor about your body, what you will put on. Is not life more than food, and the body more than clothing? Look at the birds of the air: they neither sow nor reap nor gather into barns, and yet your heavenly Father feeds them. Are you not of more value than they? And which of you by being anxious can add a single hour to his span of life? And why are you anxious about clothing? Consider the lilies of the field, how they grow: they neither toil nor spin, yet I tell you, even Solomon in all his glory was not arrayed like one of these. But if God so clothes the grass of the field, which today is alive and tomorrow is thrown into the oven, will he not much more clothe you, O you of little faith? Therefore do not be anxious, saying, "What shall we eat?" or "What shall we drink?" or "What shall we wear?" For the Gentiles seek after all these things, and your heavenly Father knows that you need them all. But seek first the kingdom of God and his righteousness, and all these things will be added to you. Therefore do not be anxious about tomorrow, for tomorrow will be anxious for itself. Sufficient for the day is its own trouble (Matthew 6:25-34, ESV).

Additionally, God grants peace that passes understanding—peace because of a clear conscience, peace because our sins have been forgiven (Acts 2:38; 22:16). We have peace that passes all understanding because we truly love others and God. We have peace because we have found the true purpose and meaning of life. We will have happiness because of the promise of heaven.

Live Today

Some are discontent and unhappy because they are stuck in the past. Others are discontent and unhappy because they live in the future. We must be in the moment to experience true contentment and happiness. Paul said, "forgetting what lies behind and straining forward to what lies ahead" (Philippians 3:13, ESV), but he lived in the moment. In 2 Timothy 1:12, he confessed, "I know whom I have believed, and am convinced that he is able to guard until that Day what has been entrusted to me" (ESV). "Sufficient for the day is its own trouble" (Matthew 6:34, ESV). Live one day at a time. Don't take on all of the mistakes of the past or the problems of the future at one time. Suppose you have a half-ton pickup truck. As long as you put a half ton on it at any one time, it will function well, but suppose you put all of the weight that truck has carried for the past ten years on it at the same time. The truck would be crushed, and so it is with us. We can't bear all of the mistakes, burdens, and guilt of the past at one time. Thank God for forgiveness, thank God He forgets about our past transgressions. Live one day at a time. Yesterday is gone, tomorrow is never promised, but I have today. Enjoy it. Be a blessing to others. Jesus said, "I am the way, and the truth, and the life. No one comes to the Father except through me" (John 14:6, ESV). Our Christian decisions definitely affect our happiness. Every decision we make will either add to or subtract from our happiness, peace, and purpose. Choose wisely.

Beyond Our Control

Having practiced as a psychotherapist for over 25 years, I understand there are conditions that affect brain chemistry and can produce depression and anxiety. We should thank God that we live in an age where psychotropic drugs can help with such conditions. How we think affects our brain chemistry. It's the old chicken versus the egg—which came first? Does incorrect thinking adversely affect our brain chemistry or does our imbalanced brain chemistry affect our thinking and disposition? I believe that there is truth in both statements. Negative, depressive, anxious thinking can affect our brain chemistry adversely. Some are born with conditions that adversely affect brain chemistry and may have to rely on medication for controlled balance. I stick by my earlier statement. Attitude, for most people, determines our happiness, peace, and contentment.

Happy Are!

God gives us a recipe for happiness. The word *"blessed"* that is used in many translations of the Beatitudes could just as easily be translated as "happy."

In Matthew 5:3-12, Jesus said, *"Happy* are the poor in spirit, for theirs is the kingdom of heaven. *Happy* are those who mourn, for they shall be comforted. *Happy* are the meek, for they shall inherit the earth. *Happy* are those who hunger and thirst for righteousness, for they shall be satisfied. *Happy* are the merciful, for they shall receive mercy. *Happy* are the pure in heart, for they shall see God. *Happy* are the peacemakers, for they shall be called sons of God. *Happy* are those who are persecuted for righteousness sake, for theirs is the kingdom of heaven. *Happy* are you when people revile you and persecute you and utter all kinds of evil against you falsely on my account, rejoice and be glad, for your reward in heaven is great, for so they persecuted the prophets who were before you."

Simple Thoughts That Help With Happiness
- Perfectionists are rarely happy because they live in an imperfect world. Learn to live with less than perfection. Accept the forgiveness that God offers for our failures.

- Not everything is absolutely black or white. We live in a world where gray exists in areas of judgment.

- Avoid addictions, obsessions, and compulsions. Practice moderation in all things. Addictions to sex, drugs and alcohol, gambling, etc. are always counterproductive to happiness.

- Develop a strong faith. "But...the one who doubts is like a wave of the sea that is driven and tossed by the wind. For that person must not suppose that he will receive anything from the Lord" (James 1:6,7, ESV).

Food For Thought

1. Do you think Christians should be happy? Why?

2. Why are some Christians not happy?

3. What are some barriers to happiness?

4. Jesus helped others. How does this quality help produce happiness?

5. Do we really believe the promises of God? Discuss Matthew 6:25-34.

6. How does Matthew 5:3-12 relate to our happiness?

7. What are some principles that help with happiness?

8. Is happiness a choice?

Building a Life
Based on Faith

"Everyone then who hears these words of mine and does them will be like a wise man who built his house on the rock. And the rain fell, and the floods came, and the winds blew and beat on that house, but it did not fall, because it had been founded on the rock. And everyone who hears these words of mine and does not do them will be like a foolish man who built his house on the sand. And the rain fell, and the floods came, and the winds blew and beat against that house, and it fell, and great was the fall of it."

Matthew 7:24-27, ESV

Inherent in each one of us there is a desire for life. This desire can be seen in every one of God's creatures. It is especially evident when life is threatened, as with the rabbit as it scurries trying to avoid the cunning fox. It can be seen, in turn, in the fox as it darts to and fro trying to avoid the elusive hounds of the hunter. To watch a person die is not a pleasant experience. On occasion, it is thrust upon us, and we must witness the breath of life fade from a loved one. At death there is usually a desperate struggle to prolong, as long as possible, the inevitable. However, just to live, to breathe—to experience the natural process of breathing and heartbeat—for man, at least, is inadequate. There must be something more. There must be a purpose for living.

There are many who suppose that life is a process of getting and processing. These are unimportant. They believe that a man's life does consist of what he possessing, the money he can acquire, the prestige he can yield, the monuments he can erect, but Christ plainly taught that a man's life does not consist of the abundance of things possessed. No, there must be more than the material aspects of life. Again, there must be a reason, a motive, and a purpose to live. In the narrative of the two builders, a comparison is made between a house and a life. All of us are builders. There is no choice. Every one of us has been given the responsibility of building a life.

A Person May Choose the Kind of Life He Wants to Build

God gives to every man a free will—the right to select the kind of life he builds. We can follow God's way and build a secure, sturdy life capable of facing the storms that may come to us, or we can follow our own direction—up one dead-end street and down another, and build an inadequate house that will crumble under the pressures of life. The choice is ours.

There are several kinds of houses a man can build. Travel approximately five miles to the right of my residence, and you will find some of the finest homes in my city. We call them mansions. They are large, stately, and more than adequate to meet most of the storms that would come to any person. Travel approximately five miles to the left, and you will find some of the worst houses in my area. We call them shacks. It takes much more planning to build a mansion; it takes a better foundation, more time and more effort to build a mansion, but the rewards are much greater and there is much room to grow. Almost anyone can build a shack. It requires little planning, little time, a shoddy foundation, and almost no effort. A shack is an unsafe structure. It is unsure, lacking in security. It is an uncomfortable kind of house and when the real storms of life come, it is inadequate for the needs. Sometimes, the collapse of the house can even result in the death of the inhabitants.

Recently I saw a sign on a house that read, "This house is unfit for human habitation." It was a dangerous house: The walls were crumbling, the plaster was falling—, and it was not the type of house in which a person would want to live. I thought there are many lives today, many bodies that are actually unfit for human habitation. I think of the sin-sick, the desperate, the addicted— when I think of these people, I immediately remember "Unfit for Human Habitation." Often, the innocent are hurt by their faulty house. The debris may strike a person simply passing by, and the innocent are often hurt as the result of an out-of-control life. It may be the result of a person striking out because of addictions, or anger, or desperation. These kinds of lives are unsure and unsafe for the people who live with them and for the people who must associate with them.

When we see the stark contrast between the mansion and the shack, I think every one of us, confronted with the choice of the kind of life we build, would want to build a mansion. Jesus says, "I am the way, and the truth, and the life" (John 14:6, ESV).

All Buildings Are Tested

We have a choice of the kind of life we build, though we do not always have the choice of the kind of environment or circumstances under which our lives are lived. The wise man built for all weather. He built for the storm and for the fair day. In good weather, both houses looked safe and adequate, but then came the test. The rain descended from above, the floods came from beneath, and the winds from the sides. From every direction, the houses were harassed. It was an impartial testing. The shack was not singled out and a heavier storm brought, but both were tested alike. All of us live in the same world and are faced with the same kinds of temptations and problems. The tests of life are truly impartial. One life, though, has the strength to withstand the storm. The other life, idly prepared, succumbs to the test.

Only One Building Can Stand

The Bible says the house of the wise man fell not. (See Matthew 7:24-25.) The character of the Christian defies the storm and the destructive forces in life. Jesus and you are a majority in any situation. With Jesus to guide and sustain you and with Christian principles undergirding your life, then you can certainly withstand the temptation and tests of life. The Bible says the foolish man's house fell, and it was a great fall for it was poorly planned and inadequately constructed. So any person's life that is founded upon a poor foundation and built with poor material will likewise fall beneath the storms of life.

We have the choice of the kind of life we want to build. We can build a sturdy, well-founded house or an inadequate, unsafe shack. The choice is ours.

Some of you may be saying, "But my life is well underway. I'm approaching middle age and older. How can I begin again to build a new life?" All of us have seen many unsafe, inadequate, dangerous shacks renovated and remodeled. These shacks, with reinforcement, a new roof, a reinforced foundation, a coat of paint, and some masonry work can become attractive, adequate, and safe houses. Remodeling is needed even in a mansion from time to time. You may need to right some wrongs, be forgiven of some sins, and determine to construct your Christian life in a better way. In fact, we may even need an urban renewal project in our lives, with reconditioning and remodeling. I promise you would change the appearance, attitude, and direction of your life if you experience such a spiritual urban renewal project. No matter how old you are, God provides a way for you to begin again. It's called a "new birth." A mansion or a shack—the choice is yours. It all begins with faith! "The fool says in his heart, 'There is no God'" (Psalm 14:1; 53:1, ESV).

Food For Thought

1. What evidences do you see that almost all men want to have better lives?

2. Discuss some life choices that affect the kind of life we build.

3. How important is the foundation of our life?

4. How can our lives become unfit for human habitation?

5. All lives are tested by storms. What makes the difference?

6. Can we start over in midlife or older? How?

Defeating

THE ENEMIES OF FAITH

Finally, my brethren, be strong in the Lord and in the power of His might. Put on the whole armor of God, that you may be able to stand against the wiles of the devil. For we do not wrestle against flesh and blood, but against principalities, against powers, against the rulers of the darkness of this age, against spiritual hosts of wickedness in the heavenly places. Therefore take up the whole armor of God, that you may be able to withstand in the evil day, and having done all, to stand.

Stand therefore, having girded your waist with truth, having put on the breastplate of righteousness, and having shod your feet with the preparation of the gospel of peace; above all, taking the shield of faith with which you will be able to quench all the fiery darts of the wicked one. And take the helmet of salvation, and the sword of the Spirit, which is the word of God;

Ephesians 6:10-17, NKJV

C an anyone deny the existence of evil? One has only to turn on the television news, read the latest edition of the newspaper, or go online and scan current events. Evil is everywhere. From those who think so little of life that they carelessly kill men, women, and children for profit or pride, to those who misguidedly think they are serving their god by destroying entire villages, taking lives in barbaric and savage ways, inflicting as much pain and suffering in the process as possible.

A friend of mine received a text recently from a concerned Christian in Atlanta, Georgia. The text was from North Africa where Christians in a particular village were rounded up, commanded to deny their faith in Jesus, and express their faith in Islam, Allah, and Muhammad, or die. The evil of Islamic extremists was seen in its purest form, as instead of killing those parents, they took the children and beheaded them in front of the parents who would not deny their faith in Jesus. Evil exists as it always has, and it can be seen in every facet of our society.

Turn on your television and see how the moral values that God has established in His Word are being mocked and ridiculed, and how every conceivable immoral act is now being labeled, and not just acceptable, but in many instances, preferable. Lifestyles that were considered abhorrent only a few years ago are now readily accepted by most, and for the minority that would object to such lifestyles there is an ample dose of persecution and rejection. The majority have succeeded in destroying absolute standards for most people. Our government, educational system, and entertainment industry are all becoming more and more evil and less righteous and moral.

How can Christians survive in a world where many are being killed because of their faith, and where others are being persecuted and devalued because of their personal commitment to the Lord? Even in the workplace, we are being silenced as to our faith. Prohibitions are being placed on our public prayers. Courts are ordering the symbols of the Christian faith to be removed from sight and sound. Satan and his minions, evil and its influence, can be seen and felt everywhere. What an incredible challenge we have as Christians to stand against such forces. But those of us who have faith in God, His Son, and the Spirit, and who believe the Bible to be His Word to man today, can find the path to survival in a world of evil.

Here is God's answer to resisting the evil of our present generation—the only successful formula for Christian victory for over two thousand years. Ephesians 6:10-18a, ESV states: "...praying at all times in the Spirit, with all prayer and supplication." Verse 10 of the same chapter gives us encouragement, "Finally, be strong in the Lord and in the strength of his might." The Lord is stronger than Satan and evil. If we don't believe that, as Christians, we may as well give up and give in to evil. God tells us how to access the power to overcome evil. "He who is in you is greater than he who is in the world," (1 John 4:4b, ESV). But to be successful, we must put on the full armor of God so that we can take a stand against the devil's schemes. God provides us the armor to withstand any assault from Satan and his evil. Without this armor, we are totally vulnerable and will be defeated in our Christian life.

Surely we realize that we live in a war zone. This earth has always been a battleground; the forces of evil and the forces of good have been and always will be battling for the hearts, souls, and minds of man. We can certainly see the evidences of Satan's influence in the lives of people who have given themselves completely to him and his way. To those who are sexually immoral, there are consequences; to those who are dishonest, there are consequences; to those who are unethical, they will suffer consequences—both here and hereafter. To the angry, violent members of society, they too, because of their sins, will find justice, sooner or later. To those who deny God, His Son, and His Word, there will be consequences. It seems that Satan is winning the war, but it has always been so. The good of the earth have always been outnumbered by the evil ones.

We are constantly reminded that we are involved in a war, as God's people. I have often felt sorry for those in war-torn parts of the world—those who live daily with the reality of physical warfare. Those of us who are Christians, however, must never forget that we too live in this war zone of life. There are those who are trying to assault us daily—our beliefs, our ideals, our convictions, our faith, we go to battle daily with Satan and his evil forces. It is easy for Christians to get battle fatigue, to feel as if we are alone and abandoned. But if we stand strong and do the will of God daily, love Him, trust Him, honor and obey Him..., we will win the ultimate victory. The shield of faith is our primary defensive piece of armor, but there are other essential pieces we must wear to be successful in this battle against evil.

Paul here encourages us to, "Be strong in the Lord and in the power of His might. Put on the whole armor of God, that you may be able to stand against the schemes of the devil. For we do not wrestle against flesh and blood, but against rulers, against the authorities, against the cosmic powers over this present darkness, against spiritual forces of evil in the heavenly places. Therefore take up the whole armor of God, that you may be able to withstand in the evil day, and having done all, to stand firm" (Ephesians 6:10-13, ESV). In order to win against the supernatural powers of evil, we must put on the spiritual armor that protects us in our walk here on this earth. Paul makes it very clear that we are going to meet with extreme resistance in our Christian life, and that each of us, as a soldier in the Lord's army, must be willing to take the armor of God. Let's put on God's armor, depend on His power and strength, and courageously do battle against evil.

Methods Satan Uses to Defeat Us

Satan is going to use every opportunity to defeat us in our quest to live for the Lord. He will create doubt in our minds, questioning whether or not what the Word teaches is true. He may even use friends and loved ones to tempt us to turn Him away, just as Job's wife tempted him to curse, and deny God. Doubt is crippling. Faith is the only answer to doubt, firm conviction and belief in what we know to be true.

Fear is another temptation. Christian cowards are useless. Those who claim to be the Lord's, yet hide and refuse to go to battle, are useless. Some may go behind monastery walls or just refuse to speak up when others are criticizing, maligning, and denying the Lord. How easy it is to sit back while others are cursing our God and, because of fear, say nothing.

Along with doubt and fear comes the triple threat of worry—worry that we might be retaliated against by Satan, worry that we're not strong enough to stay in the battle, worry that in some way we may be mentally, physically, or spiritually harmed by the fiery arrows of Satan. He never lets us forget our pasts, but constantly throws up our mistakes and failures. We must always remember that our spiritual welfare, the futures of our children and grandchildren, and those whom we love, depends upon faithful soldiers of God doing battle against evil. This battle is not with guns, knives, and bombs, but it is a battle for the hearts, minds, souls, and lives of those who are under the influence and control of Satan. It becomes a matter of us setting the proper daily example of godliness, holiness, and righteousness. It becomes a matter of us sharing why it is vitally important to seek and do the will of God.

We must share the results of living in a world where Satan is in control; where evil is constantly the norm; where there are few warriors to stand against the evil of our day; where our fellow men are deceived and destroyed on a daily basis. The armor for this battle is available—it is right in front of us. With it, we can stand and be victorious; without it, we will fall to the evil influences of Satan. This armor consists of the belt of truth, the breastplate of righteousness, the shoes ready to present the gospel of peace, the helmet of salvation, the shield of faith, the sword of the spirit, and finally, the essential quality of praying at all times, letting our prayers and requests be known to God.

Reviewing the Armor of God

The Belt of Truth. If we do not believe that our cause is just and true, we will fail from the beginning. Truth is essential. There is absolute truth. It is for us to know it and share it with all those around us. Jesus said, "I am the way, and the truth, and the life. No one comes to the Father except through Me," (John 14:6, ESV). Knowing and having complete faith in God's truth gives us the inspiration and encouragement to fight the battle. John 17:17 instructs, "Sanctify them in your truth: your word is truth" (ESV). We know that Satan is the father of lies; that he lies to us constantly; that he tells us that what is bad for us is really good for us. He encourages us to drink the poison of immorality, injustice, cruelty, and vulgarity; he is a liar—the father of all liars. We drink his poison and die a slow, painful, spiritual death. We can know the truth, and the truth will set us free. It is the truth that unshackles us from the bondage of Satan's lies. It is truth that guides us and leads us through the minefields of Satan's battlegrounds. It is the belt that holds the rest of the armor in place and keeps the soldier organized. The weak and hypocritical Christian will neglect the belt of truth and fail in his Christian quest.

The Breastplate of Righteousness. If we are not what we ask others to be, we will fail miserably and do great harm to the cause of our Lord. The breastplate of righteousness is essential. It guards all of the vital organs: the heart, the lungs, the intestines. If any of these organs are punctured, we become useless in battle, a casualty of the war.

We can never be righteous enough. "For all have sinned and fall short of the glory of God," (Romans 3:23, NKJV). Those of us who are Christians rely on the righteousness of God to cleanse us daily from our sins. Our hearts, our minds, and our souls constantly seek to be like the Father and Son, but the reality is that we will never attain such righteousness. The important part is that we desire it more than anything else. Because of that, we live more godly and righteous lives than we would by any other standard or plan. God's grace and mercy sanctify us, justify us, and cleanse us from all unrighteousness. If our hearts are protected, our minds are right. It is important that each time we stumble and fall in the battle of life that we get up, immediately dust ourselves off, and pray to God for forgiveness, strength, and His power to pursue the battle. Personal righteousness is a daily fight. Satan looks for the weak hearts, the vulnerable parts of our armor to attack us with his fiery arrows. If he ever gets to our hearts, he turns us into weak, cowering Christians or useless hypocrites. If our motives, loyalty, and actions are incorrect, then we become useless soldiers. We must put on the breastplate of righteousness, accepting the forgiveness, mercy, and grace of God. We must go forward, lifting up righteousness, godliness, and goodness to all around us as the standard of life, understanding that we must daily seek forgiveness, strengthening, and encouragement from the Lord and His Word.

Our Feet Shod in the Gospel of Peace. Ephesians 6:15 reads, "having shod your feed with the preparation of the gospel of peace" (NKJV). The Roman soldiers' shoes were very thick, with nails in the soles to help with traction. The shoes were made so the soldiers could move from left to right, up and down, quickly and with stability. Strips of leather or metal covered from the middle calf of the leg down to the shoes, giving protection. Sometimes we have to react quickly to dodge Satan's arrows. We must be sure-footed, steady, and able to move swiftly. If we lose our footing and fall, it could easily mean our spiritual death.

As Christians, it is peace we seek. We want peace of mind, peace of heart, and we pray for peace in the world, peace among nations, and peace in the family. But we know, because of Satan and his divisive nature, there will always be "wars and rumors of wars" (Matthew 24:6). Satan whispers his lies into our hearts and minds and promises "'Peace, peace!' When there is no peace!'" (Jeremiah 6:14, NKJV). When we accept Satan's way, we have anything but peace. Every day we need to be ready to share the gospel of Christ with someone. To be sharing the Word is what we are about; to be demonstrating it in our lives, as Jesus did in His, is our calling. How useless it is for us to claim to have on the breastplate of righteousness and yet to live in such a way those around us cannot see Jesus living in us. At times we walk and talk and sin and live as God's enemies do, embracing continually all of the enemy's vices. For the true soldier of God, this cannot be.

We must strap on the breastplate of righteousness and the shoes of the gospel of peace, and live as close to the Lord as possible. We know that in the moment of weakness when we fall and fail, we can and will be forgiven if we get up, pray for forgiveness, and march forward. Romans 8:1, 31-34 (ESV) encourages, "There is therefore now no condemnation for those who are in Christ Jesus....What shall we say to these things? If God is for us, who can be against us? He who did not spare his own Son but gave him up for us all, how will he not also with him graciously give us all things? Who shall bring any charge against God's elect? It is God who justifies. Who is to condemn? Christ Jesus is the one who died—more than that, who was raised—who is at the right hand of God, who indeed is interceding for us." We must have the breastplate of righteousness and the shoes of peace to guard our hearts continually. Mark 7:20-23 (ESV) states, "And he said, 'What comes out of a person is what defiles him. For from within, out of the heart of man, come evil thoughts, sexual immorality, theft, murder, adultery, coveting, wickedness, deceit, sensuality, envy, slander, pride, foolishness. All these evil things come from within, and they defile a person.'" We must guard our hearts in order to survive and to battle another day. We know that "Out of abundance of the heart the mouth speaks" (Matthew 12:34, NKJV). We understand that our bodies are the temple of God. 1

Corinthians 6:19: "Do you not know that your body is the temple of the Holy Spirit who is in you, whom you have from God" (NKJV). It is essential that we are good men and women. Luke 6:45: "A good man out of the good treasure of his heart brings forth good; and an evil man out of the evil treasure of his heart brings forth evil" (NKJV). We must keep our hearts, our motives, and our desires pure, protected by the breastplate of righteousness. Philippians 4:8 sums it up, "Finally, brethren, whatever things are true, whatever things are noble, whatever things are just, whatever things are pure, whatever things are lovely, whatever things are of good report, if there is any virtue and if there is anything praiseworthy—meditate on these things" (NKJV). We need to use this verse as a filter for everything we listen to, everything we read, everything we watch, and everything we think. Get rid of any of the impurities that are filtered through the teachings of this Scripture. As we do battle, let's try to get rid of the impurities of this life—those things that constantly bombard our senses, such as television, movies, newspapers, magazines, computers. For if we allow all of the evil of the world's standards into our lives, it will weaken us as God's solders.

The Helmet of Salvation. We must put on the helmet of salvation. Helmets are designed to protect the head. Some of the ancient helmets had ear protection so that the soldier could not hear the chilling screams during battle. The reality of salvation is essential to the Christian. We must possess the knowledge that our sins of the past are forgiven and that if our hearts, minds, and desires are correct, we will continually be cleansed by the blood of Jesus. Salvation here on earth is essential to spending eternity with God in heaven. Our salvation is our hope for the future—it is in Jesus. "Now this I say, brethren, that flesh and blood cannot inherit the kingdom of God; nor does corruption inherit incorruption. Behold, I tell you a mystery: We shall not all sleep, but we shall all be changed—in a moment, in the twinkling of an eye, at the last trumpet. For the trumpet will sound, and the dead will be raised incorruptible, and we shall be changed. For this corruptible must put on incorruption, and this mortal must put on immortality" (1 Corinthians 15:50-53, NKJV). Salvation is our hope, our prayer, our belief, our conviction. The reality of that salvation will come when we are changed into the incorruptible form that will transport the soul from here to God's eternity. First Thessalonians 4:13-17 (NKJV) teaches, "But I do not want you to be ignorant, brethren, concerning those who have fallen asleep, lest you sorrow as others who have no hope. For if we believe that Jesus died and rose again, even so God will bring with Him those who sleep in Jesus. For this we say to you by the word of the Lord, that we who are alive and remain until the coming of the Lord will by no means precede those who are asleep. For the Lord Himself will descend from heaven with a shout, with the voice of an archangel, and with the trumpet of God. And the dead in Christ will rise first. Then we who are alive and remain shall be caught up together with them in the clouds to meet the Lord in the air. And thus we shall always be with the Lord." To the victor go the spoils. Our victory in this spiritual warfare allows us the hope and the conviction of salvation through the blood of Jesus, and heaven for our home.

As faithful servants of God, we will endure much persecution and achieve battle scars in our walk through this life; but with the helmet of salvation we will always understand that the pain, suffering, and scars are worth the effort. Not that we earn our salvation in any way, but that we have done our very best to be good soldiers of the Lord and that there is laid up for us a crown of righteousness, which the Lord will give to His faithful. Scott Coltrain accurately describes it this way, "What did Jesus focus on that enabled him to endure and overcome the evil of this world? Was it the frequent and intense temptations he experienced? Was it his earthly poverty or all the verbal abuse that he suffered—the rejection and humiliation, the mocking trial and the crucifixion? Was it the physical exhaustion and torturous pain that allowed Him to be victorious in the battle with Satan?" No. As the Hebrew writer says in Hebrews 12:2, "Jesus, the founder and perfecter of our faith…for the joy that was set before Him endured the cross… and is seated at the right hand of the throne of God" (ESV). As we endure, we have the promise of being with God. That's what kept Jesus going, and it's what keeps us going. We must wear the helmet of salvation.

The Shield of Faith. "Without faith, it is impossible to please Him. The man who approaches God must have faith in two things, first that God exists and secondly that it is worth a man's while to try to find God" (Hebrews 11:6, Phillips translation).

We all know what a shield is. It protects us from incoming objects—then, arrows and spears; today, bullets and bombs. First Peter 5:8, 9 (NKJV): "…your adversary the devil walks about like a roaring lion, seeking whom he may devour. Resist him, steadfast in the faith." James 4:7 (NKJV): "Resist the devil and he will flee from you." Faith is essential. Without faith, the songs that we sing are sung in vain. Without faith, our prayers rise no higher than the ceilings. Without faith, we cannot win the battle against Satan and his minions. Strong faith sees us through all of the difficult, dark times of life. Powerful faith deflects all of Satan's attempts to destroy us. Remember how Jesus was tempted—the lust of the flesh, the lust of the eye, and the pride of life. To each of these Jesus replied, "Be gone, Satan! For it is written…." (Matthew 4:10, ESV). "Faith comes from hearing, and hearing through the word of Christ," (Romans 10:17, ESV). We must not only hear, but believe and trust the Word.

The Bible teaches us that we will never be tempted beyond what we are able to withstand. (See 1 Corinthians 10:13.) Satan is always watching us, looking for a weakness, a point of entry, a place to pierce us. But with the shield of faith strong and secure, we are safe. Read again the powerful story in 2 Kings 6:11-17. Elisha told his fearful servant as they looked at the surrounding enemy army, "'Do not be afraid, for those who are with us are more than those who are with him.' Then Elisha prayed and said, 'O Lord, please open his eyes that he may see.' So the Lord opened the eyes of the young man, and he saw, and behold, the mountain was full of horses and chariots of fire all around Elisha" (2 Kings 6:16-17, ESV). We have an unseen, powerful God who places protective angels all around us, waiting to help us. All we have to do is ask and to have faith that God will help us overcome the evil one. Do you really believe, with ultimate faith, that "all things work together for good" in your life (Romans 8:28), as you fight this incredible battle against evil? "He will not forsake you nor destroy you," (Deuteronomy 4:31, NKJV). He has given us the armor to protect us as we walk through life, battling for the souls of men. We simply have to have great faith and be constantly reminded of all of the promises of God to help us in every need of our lives; to see us through the sickness, the sadness, the sorrow, which can either become a blessing or a curse depending on who we believe—God or Satan.

How many times we wish for a truce—, an armistice, a pause in the battle—, a time to regroup, refocus, rest, and find some peace. David felt that way. Psalm 55:6-8 (NKJV) says, "So I said, 'Oh, that I had wings like a dove! I would fly away and be at rest. Indeed, I would wander far off, and remain in the wilderness. I would hasten my escape from the windy storm and tempest.'" Each of us face so many problems, difficulties, and temptations in this life and at times we go from one crisis to another, seemingly finding no time to rest and recover. But with all the promises of God and with all of the armor He provides, we will be able to make it through to the end. Then we can say with Paul, "I have fought the good fight, I have finished the race, I have kept the faith. Finally, there is laid up for me the crown of righteousness...not to me only but also to all who have loved His appearing" (2 Timothy 4:7, 8, NKJV). As you battle in life, tell God how you feel. Let Jesus know what's troubling you. Say to Him, "Lord, I feel I'm at the end of my rope. I must have some rest and encouragement." Describe to Him in detail your trials and tribulations, your needs, wants, and desires, asking for His providential help and His supernatural protection and guidance. Prayer is powerful, transforming, and essential in our quest to keep the faith.

The Sword of the Spirit. It may surprise some Christians to know that the devil knows Scripture as well as we do. He loves to twist it. He takes it out of context. He changes one or two words here and there and, as a result, deceives the heart of the Christian. The reason there is so much division, bitterness, and fighting in Christianity today is because so many have been deceived by Satan's misusing, misquoting, and misrepresenting the Word of God. There are thousands of supposed men of God who for their own personal fame or fortune twist and distort the Word of God. There are those who, for the sake of large audiences, are willing to compromise the Word of God for the applause of men. These are not men of faith, but rather followers of fable. We have to be aware that there are antichrists, false prophets, and false teachers who are leading many of God's people away from the truth (Matthew 24:11).

No man has the right to change the Word of God. It is once and for all delivered to the saints (Jude 3). Paul said, "If we, or an angel from heaven, preach any other gospel to you than what we have preached to you, let him be accursed" (Galatians 1:8, NKJV), and "Faith comes by hearing, and hearing by the word of God" (Romans 10:17, NKJV).

"Now faith is the substance of things hoped for, the evidence of things not seen....Therefore we also, since we are surrounded by so great a cloud of witnesses, let us lay aside every weight, and the sin which so easily ensnares us, and let us run with endurance the race that is set before us, looking unto Jesus, the author and finisher of our faith, who for the joy what was set before Him endured the cross, despising the shame, and has sat down at the right hand of the throne of God. For consider Him who endured such hostility from sinners against Himself, lest you become weary and discouraged in your souls....But you have come to Mount Zion and to the city of the living God, the heavenly Jerusalem, to an innumerable company of angels, to the general assembly and church of the firstborn who are registered in heaven, to God the judge of all, to the spirits of just men made perfect, to Jesus the Mediator of the new covenant, and to the blood of sprinkling that speaks better things than that of Abel....Therefore, since we are receiving a kingdom which cannot be shaken, let us have grace, by which we may serve God acceptable with reverence and godly fear" (Hebrews 11:1; 12:1-3, 22-24, 28, NKJV).

Faith is the victory that overcomes the world.

Food For Thought

1. What evil do you observe in your daily life?

2. What do you think is the greatest evil threat today?

3. What is the Christian's only hope to survive evil?

4. Can you name the pieces of Christian armor?

5. What evidences do you see that God is in control of our world?

6. Which of the pieces of armor can be used for an offensive strike?

7. Why do men want to change God's Word?

8. How did Jesus overcome the evil of this world?